LATIN AMERICA SERIES

SERIES EDITORS, SAMUEL L. BAILY and RONALD T. HYMAN

THE AFRICAN DIMENSION IN LATIN AMERICAN SOCIETIES

THE AFRICAN DIMENSION IN LATIN AMERICAN SOCIETIES

Franklin W. Knight

MACMILLAN PUBLISHING CO., INC.
NEW YORK

COLLIER MACMILLAN PUBLISHERS
LONDON

For Michael and Brian

Macmillan Publishing Co., Inc.
866 Third Avenue, New York, N. Y. 10022
Collier-Macmillan Canada Ltd.

Library of Congress Cataloging in Publication Data

Knight, Franklin W
    The African dimension in Latin American society.

    (Latin America series)
    Bibliography: p. 137
    1. Negroes in America.   2. Slavery in America.
I. Title.
E29.N3K55   301.45'19'607   73-11732
ISBN 0-02-564200-6

First Printing 1974

Printed in the United States of America

Contents

Preface to the Series

THIS SERIES OF BOOKS on Latin America grew out of a summer institute we directed at Rutgers University in 1967. The institute was sponsored by Rutgers University and supported financially by the National Defense Education Act (NDEA). We invited forty-five teachers from all over the United States to live on our campus for six weeks, to study Latin American issues, and to design with us ways of teaching these issues to their students. We also brought in leading scholars and journalists with special knowledge of Latin America to help us in our work.

These books reflect what we learned from our institute experience. The task of translating our ideas into a series of books, however, has not been easy. Two general problems have confronted us and it is well to recognize them here since their solutions have become the backbone of all of these books. First, there is the question arising from history and the social sciences: how can a person from one country or one culture adequately understand the issues facing a person from another country or another culture? The major obstacle in the path of the North American student who wishes to understand Latin America is his cultural bias. What he will learn about Latin America depends to a considerable extent upon his point of view, or his frame of reference. People see what their frame of reference prepares them to see, and most North Americans are simply not prepared to see Latin America as Latin Americans do.

A person's cultural bias or frame of reference is determined by many things including nationality, social class, religion, economic class, historical heritage, education, and technological skills. Can we in the United States—members of a highly industrialized, predominantly Protestant, democratic society—understand the people of the developing, Catholic, and for the most part authoritarian societies of Latin America? Can we whose revolution is part of the distant past sympathize with the Mexicans, Bolivians, and Cubans whose revolutions are part of the present? Is it possible for middle class, North American students to understand the life of the inhabitants of the shanty towns surrounding modern cities like Buenos Aires, Rio de Janeiro, Lima, and Santiago? Can we see the world as a variety of Latin Americans see it?

There is no simple answer to these questions. Though we may never be able to remove our own particular cultural bias, we can and must adjust our frame of reference so that we will be able to understand Latin Americans and the issues facing them. If we recognize that we have a cultural bias which determines what we see and we compare our bias with that of the people we are studying, we will have a good chance of understanding what others think and feel.

The second question concerns education: how can we meaningfully teach a person something about the issues facing people in another country? Here again there is no simple answer. We do know, however, that a person will read—and understand what he reads—when the topic is of interest to him and related to his own experience. Furthermore, we believe a reader prefers to examine those topics which call upon him to participate in the search for answers. He is not satisfied with simple, pat answers for he knows from his own experience that life is complex. Important issues are interrelated and cut across geographical areas and academic disciplines. A person is willing to participate in the search for answers, even though this approach requires a great expenditure of mental and physical effort, because this approach is meaningful and rewarding to him.

We are convinced that people will understand more about Latin America by analyzing a few key issues in depth than by attempting to learn the names of kings, viceroys, military heroes, presidents, capital cities, mountain ranges, rivers, and so forth that so often fill the pages of textbooks. We are also convinced that readers prefer—and will benefit significantly from—the study of the conflict and tension of man's affairs since these things are an important part of reality.

In summary, the books in this series will:

1. Focus on important issues rather than on a chronological coverage of Latin America.
2. Relate Latin American issues to similar issues in the United States.
3. Emphasize differing points of view to help the reader clarify his own frame of reference.
4. Emphasize controversy as a meaningful approach to the teaching of social studies.
5. Permit and encourage the reader to work with the "stuff" of Latin American studies by presenting relevant documents, maps, charts, and photographs.
6. Focus on the questions of when and how we can legitimately formulate generalizations about Latin America, whether or not we can speak of Latin America as a whole, and whether it is the similarities or the differences among the Latin American countries that are more important.
7. Discuss issues which are representative of those facing other sections of the world beside the Western Hemisphere.

The intent of the editors and authors is to present Latin America to the reader in an open-ended way. We recognize that these books can not encompass all of the important information and interpretations about the area. Our purpose is to provide a basis from which the reader can further his understanding of Latin America today.

—SAMUEL L. BAILY
RONALD T. HYMAN

New Brunswick, New Jersey
September, 1973

Chapter 1

Introduction

THIS LITTLE BOOK attempts to examine the varying pattern of social acceptance and integration of the Afro-American population throughout the countries of North and South America. It is built on several premises and seeks to answer some basic questions. These premises are (1) that the vast majority of the black population in the Western Hemisphere are the descendants of African slaves transported to the Americas between the sixteenth and the nineteenth centuries; (2) that the conditions of slavery varied equally within similar systems across the Americas; (3) that the plantation system of slavery was relatively uniform, but not identical, everywhere in the Americas; and (4) that the slave on a sugar plantation fitted into a socioeconomic and political complex that was basically similar in Louisiana, Cuba, Jamaica, St. Domingue, Surinam, and Brazil.

Why then should the postslavery Afro-American populations find such a wide variety of life and conditions from place to place in the Americas? How and why did the United States of America develop such a rigidly exclusive policy toward the

I

descendants of its slaves, with a system of laws and customs not found anywhere else? Why should racial discrimination be more manifest in the social relations of the United States of America than anywhere else in the hemisphere?

In attempting to answer these questions, we must bear in mind two things: first, that there is a historical dimension based on slavery and the legacies of the slave society that varied from place to place; second, that the social structure of present-day American societies, especially the ethnic composition of their population, has some bearing on the problem. The two considerations are interrelated. We must always bear in mind that diversity is intrinsic to the human community, as it is of all nature. No two societies, therefore, can be identical.

Africans, and people of African descent, have played a major role in the development of all American societies. This role has often been indirect, and frequently obscure. This is especially true in those parts of the Americas where the present Afro-American populations constitute a minority within their respective countries.

Africans were among the very earliest immigrants to the Americas. They were on many of the voyages of discovery, and they formed parts of all the colonies and trading posts established by the Europeans in the New World. Some of the activities of these Africans and their descendants are well known. They planted wheat and worked in the mines in Mexico. They worked on the coffee, tobacco, and sugar plantations in a very wide area of tropical America from Brazil through the Caribbean to the southern United States.

Afro-Americans, however, did more than toil on plantations. They held a wide variety of occupations, fulfilling the needs of the time and place in which they found themselves. In the very early days, some were *conquistadores*, winning along with the Spanish conquerors the highlands of Mexico and Peru for the monarchs of Castille. Later some were buccaneers throughout the Caribbean, wantonly attacking organized society and disrespecting international laws. At all times Afro-Americans herded cattle on the vast plains of the United States, Mexico, northern South America, and the Argentine. In every American society, too, these people practiced crafts and supplied needed social services, such as barbering, smithing, baking, driving coaches, or serving in the household.

Some occupations of the slaves often overlapped those of the free white and black members of the community throughout the period of slavery. Chapter 2 looks at these occupations and traces their expansion and change during the postslavery period. This chapter also relates the social and economic roles of the slaves and the free black community to the two basic patterns of colonization in the Americas: the desire to settle and the desire primarily to plant and exploit. Settler America tried to reproduce the society of the mother country; nonsettler America, sometimes called Plantation America or Exploitation America, was developed essentially to supply tropical staples for the European market. Settler America was predominantly a white society; nonsettler America became predominantly black or Indian, with Africans performing most of the work in the plantation areas.

Chapter 3 looks at the social and racial attitudes engendered by settlers and nonsettlers, and it examines the complex problem of racism between the sixteenth and the nineteenth centuries.

Chapter 4 extends the examination of racism and race relations to the twentieth century. It explores the diversity that exists among the United States, Brazil, Cuba and Puerto Rico, and the British West Indies.

Chapter 5 compares the integration of other immigrant groups with that of the Afro-Americans; chapter 6 concludes with a summary of the major factors affecting social integration throughout the Americas.

Chapter 2

The Experience of Slavery

THE EXPERIENCE OF SLAVERY profoundly influenced the spatial distribution as well as the social and political conditions of the present Afro-American population. Nevertheless, the fact that slavery provided a unifying bond ought not to obscure the vast complexity of the slavery experience, not just in the Americas but also in Africa. The African background is an important aspect of the American slave experience. It shows how the impact of the Europeans and the reality of the American situation transformed the social experience of a vast mass of people and created an entirely new society. And this entirely new society—the American slave society—provided a new experience for both Africans and Europeans. While we examine the development of this unique experience in this chapter, we shall also include the proportion of slave importation that resulted in the postslavery Afro-American population and trace the differences among the slave systems in the Americas.

Most writers have focused on differences among slave systems in terms of national boundaries. We will, however, make our divisions along more meaningful and realistic lines. We shall first make a distinction between settler America, which as we said were areas designed for permanent European settlement, and nonsettler America, which were areas designed for the production of staples and goods required by the Europeans. Within these two broad divisions we will further subdivide according to the size of slaveholdings. We call one type large-scale holdings and the other small-scale holdings; and both types overlapped in settler and nonsettler America to provide important consequences for each society and community.

The African Background

The Afro-American populations of today stem largely from the transatlantic slave trade, which operated between 1521 and 1870. This European-dominated operation accounted for the African "diaspora," or disperson. When Afro-Americans try to understand their history and their society, they look back to the slave trade that brought their ancestors to the Americas, as well as to the structure of African society from which a good part of their culture derived. The American experience was influenced by the African background.

Most Afro-Americans have always had a mystical attachment to Africa. Yet the links that connect Africa and the Americas have never been clear. The history of Africa before the arrival of the Europeans is still neglected and distorted. During the years of the slave trade, when the massive migrations from Africa took place, the conditions of entry into the Americas prohibited the establishment of any viable culture that could be distinctively called African. Nevertheless, the attachment of the Africans for their land remained very strong, and they communicated this fondness to the generations born in the Americas. Succeeding generations of African descendants learned of Africa only through this diluted process, this mystique. The mystical ideals that Afro-Americans contrived about Africa often contrast sharply with reality and produce problems for Afro-Americans who later travel there. The famous North American writer W. E. B. Du Bois confessed that although he felt very strongly about Africa, he could never adequately express those feelings. And many Afro-Americans fail to find in Africa the happiness and mental tranquillity that they had anticipated prior to their arrival there.

Yet a number of American poets and novelists have expressed beautiful images of Africa—some of them even without setting foot on African soil. We therefore owe to the writings of Claude McKay, Langston Hughes, Countee Cullen, Jean Toomer, Lucian Watkins, Aimé Cesaire, and Derek Walcott some of the best images of Africa that form part of the American cultural heritage. But the history of Africa ought to be an equally integral part of the American consciousness.

Africa has had a long and distinguished history and ancient and distinguished civilizations. Africans have been among the foremost in dominating their environment and establishing urban centers until the very recent past. Africans have domesticated grains and animals, forged weapons, and established communities that extended beyond the enlarged kinship families. In short, African community life was sophisticated before the Europeans first made contact with Africans south of the Sahara. Not all Africans knew how to write; but writing is a very recent invention, even among the Europeans. Instead of written scrolls, the Africans left their history in their sculptures and in their tools, their pyramids, and their numerous oral traditions handed down from generation to generation.

We know that Africa had an illustrious past. What is difficult to understand is why this past has been so neglected and maligned.

Part of the cause of the distortion and denigration of African history lies with the unfortunate after-effects of the transatlantic slave trade. This operation considerably altered the then prevailing power relations in the world, putting Africa at a considerable disadvantage. When the Europeans first made their exploratory voyages along the African coast during the late fifteenth and early sixteenth centuries, they did not immediately think of the Africans as inferior to themselves. They realized that they were different from Europeans, but they accepted them as their equals. However, the results of conquest and the manpower requirements of an expansive

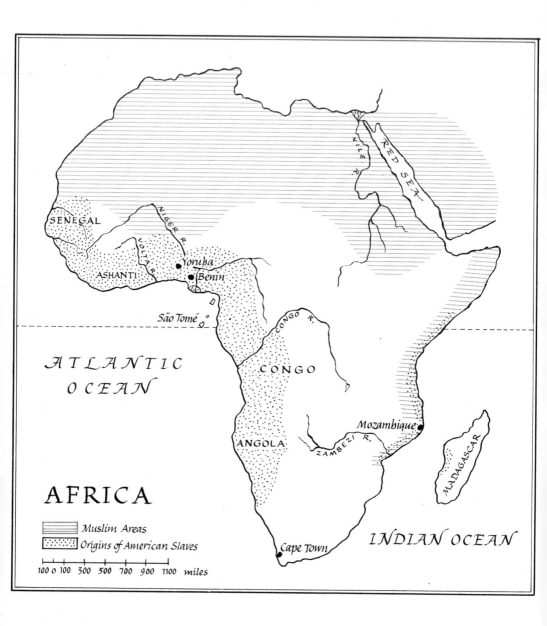

SENEGAL

ASHANTI

Yoruba

Benin

São Tomé

NIGER R.

VOLTA R.

NILE R.

RED SEA

CONGO R.

CONGO

ANGOLA

Mozambique

ZAMBEZI R.

MADAGASCAR

ATLANTIC
OCEAN

Cape Town

INDIAN OCEAN

AFRICA

▦ Muslim Areas
▨ Origins of American Slaves

100 0 100 300 500 700 900 1100 miles

European imperialism demoted Africa in the eyes of Europeans. Imperialism created two worlds: Europe and non-Europe.

But the Europeans did not begin the slave trade. Before the fifteenth century, Africans had already established the techniques of uprooting men and expelling them from their native villages. Slavery, albeit in a different form, existed in Africa before the arrival of the Europeans. The increased demand for men to work in the Americas radically changed the structure of African slavery, and the domestic trade blended into the transatlantic slave trade in which Europeans and Africans became coequal partners.

AFRICAN SLAVERY: MUSLIM AND NON-MUSLIM

The indigenous systems of African slavery were fundamentally different from those that later developed in the Americas. The African slave systems fell into two basic divisions, Muslim and non-Muslim. Although the structural differences were not very great, the religious, cultural, and political homogeneity of the Muslim area gave slavery a certain distinctiveness that it lacked in non-Muslim Africa.

Muslim Slavery

In Muslim Africa, as elsewhere throughout the Islamic world, the sanction for slavery came from the duty of the faithful to convert all nonbelievers, by persuasion if possible, or by force if necessary. Of course, it was usually easier to convert with the sword or, later, the gun. However they were acquired, Muslim slaves were accepted into the household and assumed the status of a child, or a ward. Indeed, kinship terms were frequently used between masters and slaves.

The laws of the Koran obliged all masters to educate their slaves. This had important repercussions on the structure of the society. It meant that although the slave became a dependent, he was never so low in social status that he could not rise in the world through service to his master. Indeed, slaves could get out of slavery and become important persons in free society without any stigma whatsoever. In many parts of Muslim North Africa, the military forces, such as the janissaries, were created by purchasing slaves. Often, especially in Egypt and Morocco, slaves dominated politics and became the self-perpetuating rulers of the country.

Non-Muslim Slavery

Outside the spheres of Muslim influence, the pattern of slavery was similar to that of Muslim North Africa. While there was no religious injunction, as in the Muslim areas, the slaves became members of the family and the community, and their offspring became fully free members of the society. As a broad generalization it would be fair to say that to the south of the desert, slavery fulfilled the sociological function of group ascription. This means that enslavement served to increase the population of the community rather than to acquire a subordinate caste of permanent workers.

Throughout Africa, therefore, slaves tended to do what other members of the society did. As time passed and the trade in slaves expanded, states, such as Benin, developed based almost solely on slave raiding. Most of these states were themselves slaveholding communities. Within these states, the status of the local slaves and of those slaves captured for commercial reasons was quite distinct. Some states even used slaves as the commanders of the expeditions that went out to raid slaves for commerce. This benign form of slavery did not survive the impact of European trade with the Africans.

THE IMPACT OF THE EUROPEANS ON AFRICA

The first impact of the Europeans on African society south of the Maghreb came with the formation of the Portuguese post off the Sahara coast at Arguin, around 1443. This was part of the scheme of Portuguese and European expansion into the wider world to reduce the religious threat to Europe from Islam and to undermine the commercial position of the Maghrebi middlemen in gold and slaves. The trading post at Arguim was still far from the real source of gold and slaves, and it was too far north in the savanna zone. Yet it was strategically located to intercept the trade in gold that had flowed northward from the upper Niger region around Wangara to the North African Muslim states. Although Arguin succeeded in serving as an exchange center for the trade in salt, gold dust, and slaves, it failed to undermine the Maghrebi commercial position. Therefore the Portuguese pressed on down the African coast.

By 1482 the Portuguese had established a trading fort at El Mina on the Gold Coast of West Africa and tried hard to maintain a garrison of about sixty men to protect their trade goods. At this time the coastal peoples of this part of Africa were divided into small, warring states. Nevertheless, none of them was small enough or weak enough to afford the Portuguese an opportunity to establish a foothold on the mainland. After all, the Europeans were not always superior to Africans in land fighting, and they preferred not to challenge the Africans on their home territory.

The fort on El Mina was constructed under the sufferance of the coastal peoples who seemed anxious enough to trade with the Europeans. But the peoples of the coast had no slaves to trade at that time. They had gold, however, and so the Portuguese transshipped most of the slaves bought at Arguin to El Mina, where they exchanged them for gold. In the fifteenth century the demand for slaves was still low. The slave-worked plantations had barely reached the Iberian Peninsula, and the tropical Atlantic islands of São Tomé and Fernando Po had not yet developed slave systems.

As the Portuguese continued along the tropical West African coast they found that a new strain of malaria decimated their non-immune adult population at an alarming rate. In fact, the initial death rate varied between 25 percent and 75 percent of those infected. The Africans who were born in the area, and who survived infancy, had an apparent immunity that lasted as long as they lived in the region. In order to carry on any kind of activity, therefore, the Europeans would have to pay the price of the death of more than half of all the personnel they brought to the coast. It was not a pleasing prospect, and it discouraged whatever vague ideas of conquest the Portuguese might have had. In addition, those Europeans who survived malaria faced the threat of yellow fever. Until the late nineteenth century, therefore, Europeans in West Africa faced double jeopardy: death by malaria, or death by yellow fever.

Yet the commercial advantages of gold forced the Europeans to hazard the problems to their health. After all, those who got the bulk of what wealth was derived from these regions were usually safe away in Europe. The Portuguese persevered, driven by the desires of God, gold, and glory.

When the Portuguese advance reached São Tomé and Fernando Po, they found that sugar plantations could be profitable business. But sugar plantations demanded more manpower than Portugal could provide. Moreover, there was a double advantage in using African slaves: They were cheaper, and they lasted longer against the hazards of the environment. The Portuguese began to develop a demand for slaves as well as gold.

By the time the plantations of São Tomé were fully established, the Portuguese trading empire had reached Asia, and Portugal was able to provide a wide variety of products that Africans were willing to buy, products ranging from firearms to spices. On the other hand, the expanding African states that were conducting military expeditions along their borders found that the Portuguese were anxious to buy their prisoners of war. The vicious cycle had begun. The Africans' demand for imported products accentuated their desire to wage wars in order to find prisoners to sell. Soon other excuses would be found to sell their fellowmen to foreign traders.

The process of organizing this trade followed a trial-and-error basis. South of the Congo River, the Portuguese found one kind of situation at their arrival where the most important kingdom in a fluid situation was the kingdom of Congo. The Congolese king, in order to bolster his political position, converted to Christianity and made a treaty with the Portuguese in which he gave them a monopoly over the foreign trade in return for their support against other non-Christian Africans. As time went on, the Portuguese support became vital for the kings of the Congo. This support gradually developed into informal Portuguese control, not only over the Congo but also over the neighboring states in the hinterland of Luanda. Therefore, the Portuguese had a vast area from which they could draw slaves without keeping a large military force on land.

North of the equator, the Portuguese found another situation in the Bight of Benin. The Portuguese maintained a station at Gwato, the port of Benin, but the Oba, or King, was strong, and the kingdom well-organized. The Oba rejected the Portuguese offer to convert to Christianity. Benin had a substantial source of prisoners from its expanding wars in the region of the mouth of the Niger. The Binis of Benin and the Portuguese found that they could strike a mutually rewarding bargain by exchanging prisoners for European goods. The prisoners thus purchased through the Portuguese factory at Gwato between 1486 and 1515 went partly to El Mina to pay for gold exports, partly to Europe, where they fitted into domestic and other services, and partly to São Tomé and Fernando Po to work on sugar plantations.

The Portuguese pattern became the model for the other Europeans. The Portuguese naval mobility had two consequences. In the first place, they found that they could very profitably buy slaves along the Guinea coast without having any formal type of control or establishing sizable settlements that would become a prey to malaria and yellow fever. In the second place, the coastal peoples found that the Europeans were keen on purchasing slaves, and so they began a slow, subtle transformation of their domestic economies to supply the Europeans with what they wanted. The methods started by the Portuguese in the late fifteenth century became standard among all Europeans when the transatlantic slave trade became a booming business during the seventeenth century. This change was evident in El Mina, which began as an import point for slaves and ended up as one of the most lucrative export stations for Africans in the history of the slave trade.

The transatlantic slave trade greatly modified the existing societies and institutions of Africa and mobilized large numbers of Africans to work in slave gangs on the type of capitalist-operated plantations that spread from southern Iberia to the Americas.

Europeans and the African Slaves

One of the curious observations about African slavery in the New World is that the Europeans who introduced and developed it no longer practiced slavery at home. The medieval European system of serfdom had been fading fast, with vestiges remaining only in the eastern lands. In Iberia, a significant proportion of the Africans were free men in free associations—some even participating in the then rapidly rising, popular sport of bullfighting. But plantation slavery using Africans had existed on the foothills of Malaga in Spain and in the Algarve region of Portugal in the early fifteenth century. Before the Portuguese had begun to tap the sub-Saharan source of slaves at Arguin, there was an association of African freedmen in Barcelona. Although Europeans in general had not been enslaving their fellowmen at home, they were (especially the Italians and the Iberians) quite familiar with slavery and African slavery after the crusades to the Holy Land. Yet of paramount importance was the fact that no labor shortage existed in Europe—hence the low figures of Africans being sent to Europe. Things were different in the New World.

The discovery of the New World opened up nearly 16 million square miles of new territory to the Europeans. This area was many times the size of Europe. The Spaniards, who were the first to burst upon this vast preserve, could do little more than settle small enclaves in the 100 years before the other Europeans began to make permanent settlements. In 1500, the entire population of Europe was perhaps less than 100 million—or a little more than twice the present population of the British Isles. This meant that in a total land area of some 3.7 million square miles, the European population had an average density of about 27 persons per square mile. Spain at that time had probably less than 4 million people spread over its slightly less than 200,000 square miles. Whether the Europeans realized it or not, their expansion into this new American territory was bound to affect their lives and institutions seriously by reducing further the ratio of men to the land.

The initial Spanish aim in the New World was to seek trade

and to convert the peoples of the Americas to Christianity while subjecting them to the monarchy of Castille. The first Spaniards who came to the New World brought the ideals of the aristocratic, aggressive Castilian nobility, "oriented toward warfare and the gain of riches by warfare." Even the Castilian peasants came with a desire for free land and quiet wealth and the leisured life based on the exploitation of Indian labor. Since gold could not be had in the quantities desired, the Spaniards found that they somehow had to work the land, but they concentrated on grazing and mining. When the Spaniards themselves refused to do the demanding physical labor (and the local Indian population declined catastrophically from a number of causes), they turned to importing African laborers as slaves. Ideas of bilateral trade gave way to the desires of an exploitation colony.

For the Spanish colonists in the Americas of the sixteenth century, the problem was mainly one of organizing the available labor to produce the types of commodities that could be exported profitably to Europe. Slavery offered the most desirable system of labor organization, since it allowed the master to control almost absolutely the life and productivity of the slave. Indian slavery, however, proved unsuccessful both in the Antilles and on the mainland. In a short time the Spaniards were without their desired services. Attempts to recruit the laborers from Spain met with total fiasco: Those who came wanted to be independent and free men. Spain turned to Africa for the workers she needed, but she was unable to recruit locally. Unfortunately, from the Spanish point of view, Spain and Portugal had already signed the Treaty of Tordesillas in 1494, thereby denying Spanish access to Africa. At the time, neither country realized how important Africans would be in the development of their American exploitation colonies.

Slavery, therefore, became the medium for restricting the mobility of men on the land and for controlling their efforts toward the production of specific items. The Americas presented an area of "open resources" to the Europeans; every man arriving there could wander off beyond the frontier of organized society. Some Europeans and Africans undoubtedly did just that and became transfrontiersmen: western mountain men, buccaneers, maroons, gauchos. But the majority preferred to stay together in their settled colonial enclaves. Settlement presupposed and necessitated division of labor, and the easiest solution for accomplishing arduous and unpleasant labor was to bring in outsiders to do it. The outsiders came from Africa.

The two principal reasons for the use of slavery were the unavailability of free labor and the lower cost of, and greater control over, unfree labor. Slavery tied men to the land—an important consideration if the American colonies were to be a success. Where sufficient local inhabitants survived in parts of Central Mexico and the Peruvian highlands, the Spanish used forms of coercion such as the *encomienda, repartimiento*, and *mita* to force the Indians to work for them. But elsewhere in the Americas, the Portuguese in Brazil and the English and the French in the Caribbean and North America found that the local populations were insufficient to provide adequate slaves. The Portuguese, English, and French, therefore, either disregarded the natives or exterminated them and brought Africans to do the work.

The demand for Africans, however, came only when the American colonists began to produce plantation crops for export to the European markets. Until the early seventeenth century the demand for tropical staples in Europe was relatively low. Most colonists in the Americas outside the lucrative Spanish mining districts were barely surviving in a marginal way. Their efforts were concentrated toward food production. Most colonists, therefore, shared the work with their indentured servants or with the slaves of those fortunate enough to have them. Until production in Virginia swamped the market, tobacco was the major cash crop, with cotton important in some places. Farms tended to be small, seldom exceeding thirty-five acres. As the North American colonies developed, the pattern of settlement in the Americas changed. The tropical lowlands and islands became the cradle of plantation agriculture—and plantation agriculture thrived on the strength of imported African labor.

The early history of Barbados clearly emphasized the changing nature of land use and colonial society in the New World—at least in those areas where slavery and the plantation society predominated. Barbados was one of the first settlements made by a non-Iberian state in the New World. In 1642, seventeen years after permanent settlement was made, Barbados had a population of about 15,000 persons. More than 11,000 persons were property holders, called freeholders. The island of 166 square miles was a haven for the yeoman farmer who survived on maize and tobacco.

By 1642, however, Virginia-produced tobacco and Carolina-produced cotton had virtually destroyed the economic base of Barbados. The island was saved by the agricultural conversion to sugar cane, introduced by the Dutch from Brazil. The population figures tell the story of the rapid conversion. By 1645 the white population had increased to 40,000, and the Africans, who numbered a few hundred in 1642, had increased to more than 6,000. In 1685 the white population had declined to about 20,000, while the African slave population had increased to more than 46,000. After that, the African population stabilized for a while, as the Europeans moved out to establish plantations in other islands or to become landed proprietors in the mainland colonies. The experience of Barbados was repeated in most of the other island colonies of the English and French as large estates absorbed small parcels and slaves replaced free men. The initial settlement colonies yielded to plantation colonies of sojourning whites and enslaved Africans.

SLAVERY AND EUROPEAN CAPITALISM

The history of slavery is closely tied to the growth of European capitalism. The contribution that slavery made toward the rise of European capitalism lies in the recognition of the slave trade as a branch of European commerce at the time. The slave trade from Africa to the New World and the commerce involving the products of slave-operated plantations in the tropics composed what is called the South Atlantic System.

The South Atlantic System was a complex system of trade and migration, involving capital, ships and manufactured goods from Europe, African labor, and a variety of tropical and nontropical staples grown in colonies found primarily in tropical America. These staples included tobacco (which could be successfully grown outside the tropics), sugar cane (which could not), cotton, indigo, dyewood, and spices. Sugar cane and tobacco were the most important products by far. And African slaves were the most important single element. Moreover, the Africans became the largest immigrant group of people in the world before the nineteenth century with its improved technology, improved transportation facilities, and increased populations worldwide.

During the four centuries between 1451 and 1851, approximately 9 million Africans arrived throughout the New World. Of this total, approximately 427,000 came to the British North American colonies, which later became the United States of America, and all but about 50,000 came before the legal abolition of the slave trade by Great Britain in 1808. About 1.5 million Africans went to all parts of Spanish America, with the majority of them going to Cuba and Puerto Rico after the late eighteenth century. Brazil alone imported more than 3.5 million Africans before 1870. The French Caribbean and Circum-Caribbean colonies—Saint Domingue, Martinique, Guadeloupe, Louisiana, and French Guiana —imported some 1.6 million; while the English Caribbean —Jamaica, Barbados, the Windward and Leeward Islands, Trinidad, Tobago, and Guiana—imported about the same number. In addition, Africans went to the small Caribbean islands of the Dutch and the Danes, as well as to Europe. These places received small numbers, however, and were not full participants in the South Atlantic System complex.

What is important about this massive migration of Africans is that they went as commercial assets, as slaves, and that they went unknowingly and involuntarily. The volume of this trade has been measured and examined by Professor Philip D. Curtin of the University of Wisconsin. He found that there was a pattern of growth to the trade. It began with a trickle to Europe in the fifteenth century, increased to an annual average of about 2,000 by 1600; 13,000 by 1700; 55,000 by 1810; and thereafter declined sharply until the termination of the trade in 1870. But like all trade, the operation fluctuated widely. There were periods of sharp decline in activity, especially during the years in which the European nations were at war, followed by periods of boom, when peace promoted agricultural expansion and stimulated market demands in Europe.

A direct connection between the transatlantic slave trade and the growth and prosperity of the American plantation colonies is obvious. In the seventeenth century, Barbados was the most valuable British colony, and Barbados received the greatest number of African slaves. By the eighteenth century, the tide had changed to the English colony of Jamaica and the French colony in St. Domingue. Just before the French Revolution of 1789, St. Domingue was the most valuable colony in the world, handling more than two-thirds of French foreign trade. St. Domingue produced sugar, tobacco, indigo, and a little cotton—all on plantations owned by Europeans or persons of European extract; and all the plantations were worked almost exclusively by the labor of some 480,000 African and Afro-Caribbean slaves. Some historians refer to the eighteenth century as the days when sugar was "king," when fortunes were made and lost, and when those small, beautiful Caribbean islands were the envy of the European powers, especially the English, and the French.

The connection between the South Atlantic System and the rise of capitalism in Europe is less obvious. Nevertheless, the South Atlantic System was both the cause and the result of the extremely complex operation of trade, finance, and capital accumulation that eventually gave birth to the Industrial Revolution. Contemporaries found no difficulty in making the connection, however hesitant later historians have been. An English knight wrote: "The pleasure, glory and grandeur of England has been advanced more by sugar than by any other commodity, wool not excepted." Adam Smith remarked that "our tobacco colonies send us home no such wealthy planters as we see frequently arrive from our sugar islands." Cuba only became "the jewel in the Spanish Crown" when it was the single largest producer of sugar in the world and the most important contributor to the Spanish treasury during the nineteenth century.

The most obvious result of the slave trade and the South Atlantic System can be seen in the phenomenal growth and

Manumission of a slave before the Revolution. Frontispiece of Voyage a l'ile Bourbon, of Bernardin de Saint-Pierre, by Moreau le Jeune.

Racial Equality proclaimed by the Declaration of Rights of Man (August 1789) and the decree of May 15, 1791.

Chevalier de Saint Georges, brilliant violinist, composer, and fencer acclaimed under the Monarchy, commanding colonel in 1791 of the famous regiment of Negroes and mulattoes: The American Legion.

Toussaint Louverture, commander-in-chief of the French Army of the island of Saint-Dominque, and governor of the island.

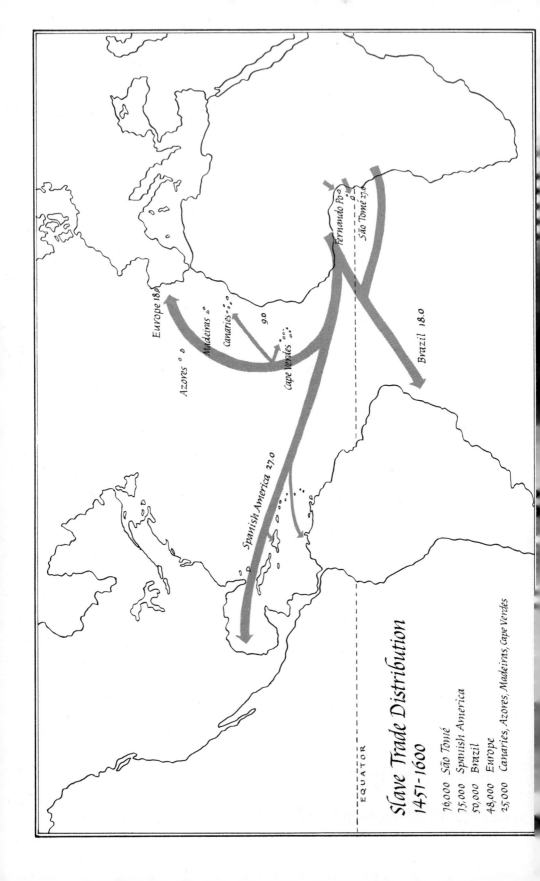

Slave Trade Distribution
1451-1600

76,000 São Tomé
75,000 Spanish America
50,000 Brazil
48,000 Europe
25,000 Canaries, Azores, Madeiras, Cape Verdes

Europe 18.0

Azores o ᵈ

Madeiras o ᵒ

Canaries ᵒᵒ

9.0

Cape Verdes

Brazil 18.0

Fernando Po

São Tomé 27.0

Spanish America 27.0

EQUATOR

prosperity of the European port cities most associated with the trade: Amsterdam, The Hague, Nantes, Bordeaux, London, Bristol, Liverpool, and Glasgow. Eric Williams in his book *Capitalism and Slavery* has meticulously traced the rise of English capitalism during the age of mercantilism to the expansion of slavery and slave trade. Mercantilism, of course, was the set of political and economic policies used by the various European powers in the seventeenth and eighteenth centuries to regulate and monopolize the trade and commerce of their states and colonies. By measures made explicit in a series of navigation laws that decreed that all goods to the colonies must be sent in ships belonging to the mother country, the metropolis dominated the export and import trade of the colony.

According to Williams, the first major stimulus from the slave and sugar business came in the sphere of shipbuilding and shipping. The operation of the slave trade required a large number of ships, and so the shipbuilding capacity of a port such as Liverpool expanded proportionately to the demand created by the African and transatlantic slave trade. A little more than 50 percent of English ships and nearly one-half of all English sailors and English naval tonnage were engaged in the sugar trade between Britain and the Antillean islands, mainly Barbados, in 1690. The involvement increased even more during the eighteenth century. During that time, British ships clearing for Africa—not all of which were involved in the slave trade—increased twelvefold. In 1774, it was claimed that almost every person living in Liverpool participated in some way in the South Atlantic System. Between 1770 and 1773 the population of the town increased from 5,000 to more than 34,000, making Liverpool one of the most populous and wealthy ports of England. By 1790 about 138 ships left Liverpool for Africa. But the financial crash came hard in 1808 with the abolition of the English slave trade. Liverpool lost an estimated £7.5 million, or $37.5 million at the rate of exchange then. In 1808, that was an enormous sum of money.

The economic history of Liverpool was repeated for Bristol, although Bristol owed most of its wealth in the eighteenth century to the sugar trade with the West Indian islands. With certain variations, the French Atlantic port cities of Nantes and Bordeaux owe their economic growth and importance to

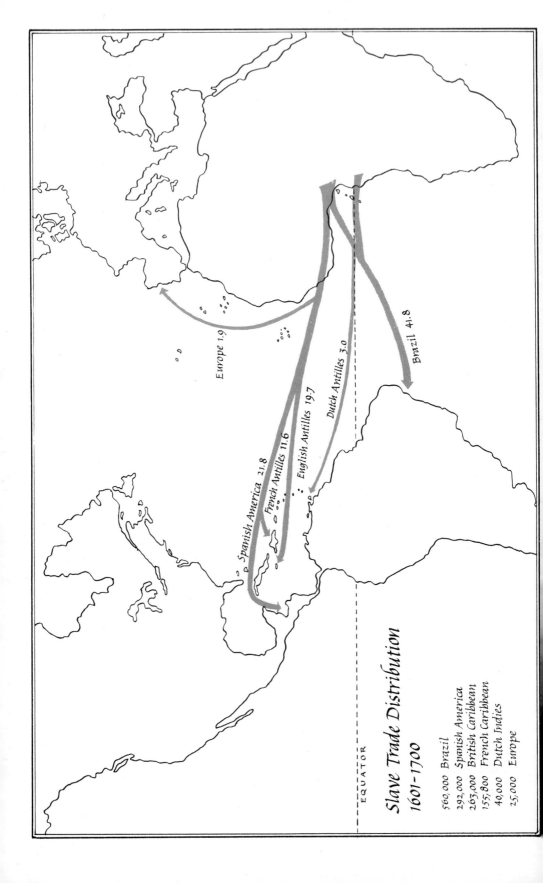

Europe 1.9

Brazil 41.8

Spanish America 21.8

French Antilles 11.6

English Antilles 19.7

Dutch Antilles 3.0

EQUATOR

Slave Trade Distribution
1601–1700

560,000 Brazil
292,000 Spanish America
263,000 British Caribbean
155,800 French Caribbean
40,000 Dutch Indies
25,000 Europe

the French part of the transatlantic slave trade and the trade in tropical staples from its Caribbean colonies.

It was not only in slavery and plantation-derived products that money was invested and capital accumulated. Rather it was also in the associated industries, such as textiles, ironware, machinery, and luxury items, that arose to service the slave trade and the slave-run plantations. This associated industrial development produced the seeds of the later Industrial Revolution. One can realize the impact that slavery and the South Atlantic System had on European and American industrial development by considering the commodities involved in the trade.

Any ship trading off the African coast would have a widely varied cargo. Such a cargo would include any or all of the following articles: cotton cloths, linen cloths, silk handkerchiefs, woolen cloths, hats and caps, umbrellas, firearms, gunpowder, lead and iron bars, pewter ware, copper kettles and pans, ironware, glass and earthenwares, beads, ornaments and rings of gold and silver, leather cases, tobacco, salt, and alcoholic spirits. The cargo was taken to the European forts and commercial stations, called factories, along the African coast. There a complicated system of bartering and haggling took place as the Africans sought to exchange their products for those the Europeans had brought. What the Africans had in abundance, especially during the eighteenth and early nineteenth centuries, were their own fellowmen whom they were consciously and unconsciously condemning to slavery. But the important observation is that a vast production network arose in Europe to provide the cargoes of those ships that sailed to Africa. Indeed, the iron industry alone, which fit the ships with chains and shackles, would have been a very extensive one. The industrial base of such inland towns as Manchester, Sheffield, Nottingham, Derby, and Birmingham derived great stimulus from the English slave trade and the English slave plantation colonies.

The North Americans were not as actively engaged in the slave trade as the English and the French. But they had just as great an interest in the slave and plantation colonies of the Caribbean. Despite the great displeasure of the English, and despite the attempts of the English Parliament to control the trade within its imperial possessions, the English North American colonists persisted in a free trade in the Caribbean until 1776. The planters of the Caribbean, regardless of whose imperial system they represented, depended upon certain products that only the Americans could supply adequately. New England and New York merchants supplied the islands with timber, grain, fish, meat, barrel staves, and horses. During the nineteenth century a great deal of the industrial equipment for Cuban sugar plantations came from the United States.

TABLE 1 *Trade Relations in Plantation America*

AREA	MAJOR EXPORTS	MAJOR IMPORTS
British North America (U.S.A.)	horses, flour, meat, codfish, barrel staves, nails, lumber, machinery, tools, firearms	sugar, molasses, spices, cash
British Antilles	slaves, cash, sugar, molasses	slaves, horses, flour, meat, fish, barrel staves, nails, lumber, tools
French Antilles	sugar, molasses, spices, coffee	slaves
Spanish Antilles	cash, tobacco, hides, sugar	slaves, firearms

Many American trading vessels sailed to the Caribbean loaded with a mixed cargo of supplies (see accompanying chart). The first ports of call were usually the English islands, where part of the cargo was exchanged for slaves, sugar, molasses, and other local produce. The vessels then moved on to the French and Spanish islands where the price of slaves was high but the price of molasses and sugar lower than in the English islands. Slaves bought in the English islands, therefore, brought a quick profit in the other islands, while staples from the latter were later resold as the higher-priced equivalents from within the empire. While this description is generally applicable, it is difficult to say that any exact pattern of trade existed. Merchants were in the business to get money, and so they did not particularly care for the niceties of imperial regulations. Even when the English and the French were at war—as they were for much of the eighteenth century—the English North American colonists conducted their trade with the French islands. During the Seven Years' War, between 1756 and 1763, some of these islands changed hands, as did Martinique and Guadaloupe, thereby facilitating the English traders. But such changes did not matter much to either the mainland merchants or their island clients. The important thing was that both sides got what they wanted from the illicit commercial operation.

Strong economic motives existed for the perpetuation and exploitation of slavery and the transatlantic slave trade both for the Western Europeans and their settler offspring in the mainland Americas. American slavery and the slave trade provided the most powerful lubricants for commerce and industry before the age of the Industrial Revolution. Much of the capital for that massive technological advance came from the accumulated profits of the South Atlantic System and its commodities of African slaves and tropical American staples. By the nineteenth century, however, the market for Antillean sugar collapsed, and the slave trade gave way to other forms of commerce. Industrializing Europe looked for new areas for their raw materials and new markets for their finished products. The new method of exploitation did not require slaves but rather new forms of imperial and economic control. The economic vulnerability of slavery became exposed: The Europeans began to reconsider their attitudes toward slavery.

EUROPEAN ATTITUDES TOWARD SLAVERY

The motives that propelled each European power into the wider world affected the early formation of its slave system. In the world of the fifteenth century, when most exploration and colonization was done by the Iberians, religion and tradi-

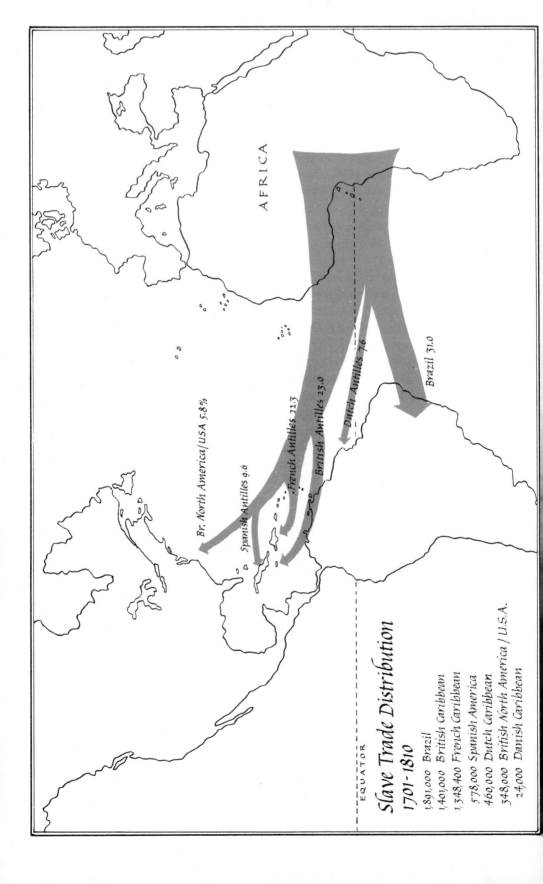

AFRICA

EQUATOR

Br. North America/USA 5.8%

Spanish Antilles 9.6

French Antilles 22.3

British Antilles 23.0

Dutch Antilles 7.6

Brazil 31.0

Slave Trade Distribution
1701–1810

1,891,000 Brazil
1,401,000 British Caribbean
1,348,400 French Caribbean
578,000 Spanish America
460,000 Dutch Caribbean
348,000 British North America / U.S.A.
24,000 Danish Caribbean

tion were still vital parts of the European heritage. Men at that time did not see a conflict between idealism and reality or religious and secular enterprises. Vasco da Gama, the Portuguese explorer, admitted that the quest for "Christians and spices" had drawn him and his frail ship to India. The loquacious Bernal Díaz del Castillo, the companion of Hernando Cortés, frankly declared that his companions went to the Indies "to serve God and His Majesty, to give light to those who were in darkness, and to grow rich, as all men desire to do." By the time the northwest Europeans ventured seriously into the non-European world of the seventeenth century, they had lost the Iberian concern for God. Religion was not an integral part of the fabric from which English, French, Dutch, and Danish colonies were cut.

The Spaniards, the first to introduce Africans as slaves in the Americas, were also the first to have a codified system of slave laws, which governed both the indigenous Indians and the imported Africans. At the time that the Spaniards established their American empire, the Spanish laws reflected the strong moral and philosophical tradition that guided the Castilian monarchs in Iberia. This legal and moral tradition permeated Spanish imperial theory, and the Spanish slave laws—as all other laws for the Indies—had to conform to this tradition. Spanish lawyers and churchmen were interested both in acting legally and morally and in seeing that their sovereign did likewise.

During the sixteenth century, Spain defined its attitude toward non-Spaniards, especially the Africans and Indians. Events occurred that clarified the Spanish position. The first was the ruling by the Pope in Rome called *Sublimis Deus*, which declared in 1537 that it was heretic to claim that non-Castilians were not rational people capable of salvation. Next, the Spanish king, Charles V, passed a series of New Laws in 1542 in which he tried to impose the authority of the monarchy over the Spanish citizens in the New World. At the same time he sought to protect the Indians—a measure that could be extended also to the Africans. The New Laws resulted in a civil war in Peru and colonial discontent almost everywhere else, and so a number of the laws were rescinded. But the New Laws showed the concern of the monarchy in

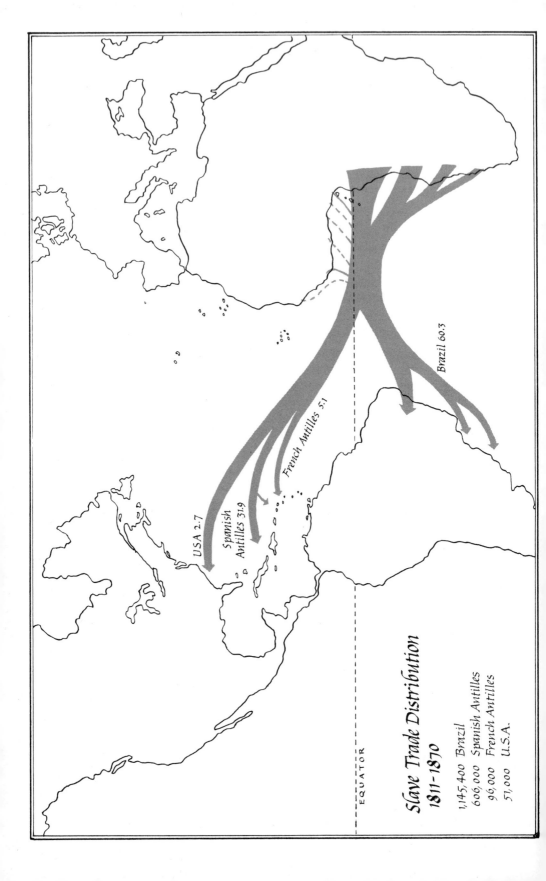

Slave Trade Distribution
1811-1870

1,145,400 Brazil
606,000 Spanish Antilles
96,000 French Antilles
51,000 U.S.A.

Brazil 60.3

French Antilles 5.1

Spanish Antilles 31.9

USA 2.7

EQUATOR

establishing a legal and just system of relationship between masters and slaves in the Americas. Finally, in the years 1550–1551, a celebrated series of debates took place at Valladolid, about 120 miles north of Madrid, between the Dominican clergyman, Bartolomé de las Casas, the so-called "Protector of the Indians," and the outstanding Spanish lawyer, Juan Ginés de Sepúlveda.

Las Casas argued that wars against the Indians to enslave them were "perverse and tyrannical." He went on to say that all men were equal and that the Spaniards had no right to the Americas. The Spanish Crown, he advised, should only send missionaries and specially selected men who would work the land and teach the Indians the Castilian customs and the Roman Catholic religion. With logic, foresight, and passion, Sepúlveda replied that the Spaniards had both a right and a duty to enslave and "civilize" the Indians, that all men were not equal, and that some men were naturally slaves. For the time being, however, the Crown accepted the view of Las Casas. In this way, the Spanish Crown and the Roman Catholic Church became identified in principle with tolerance, humanitarianism, and paternalism.

The official acceptance of the position advocated by Las Casas did not mean that the imperial bureaucracy would minutely scrutinize the actual relations between masters and slaves. But at least it created avenues for institutional intervention. And from time to time, laws governing slavery and the colonial society were handed down. In 1680 the first attempt was made to gather together these laws, the first of many such efforts issued as the *Recopilación de las leyes de los reynos de las Indias,* or "Collection of Laws for the Kingdoms of the Indies." A great part of these regulations concerned public order, slave rebellions, and the Spanish attempts at the stratification and racial separation of the colonial society. The laws, however, did not prevent abuses from time to time and from place to place throughout the empire. Each part of the empire worked out its own solution to the problem of race and the position of the black man.

The Portuguese, like the Spanish, were also a crusading people. The Portuguese had "a seaborne empire cast in a military and ecclesiastic mold." This seaborne empire varied considerably from simple trading stations, such as Goa and Macao, to settlement colonies, such as Brazil. In general, Portuguese relations with non-Portuguese tended to follow the pattern of Spain, although the Portuguese were far less legalistic about things.

When the French, the English, and the Dutch began to establish their American empires, they did not have the elaborate legal and moral tradition of the Iberians. For one thing, these countries lacked the frontier experience with the Moors, which was part of the Iberian heritage. For another, they began their imperial expansion much later. By the seventeenth century the northwest Europeans had broken the monolithic hold of Roman Catholicism, and they had either gained local control of their own church or had established independent churches. In any case, they did not have the same proselytizing zeal that had been part and parcel of the Portuguese and Spanish effort in imperial expansion.

Unlike the Spanish, who attempted to convert and accommodate the Indians of the Antilles, the English in Virginia and New England thought the Indians to be beyond the pale of salvation. Nor did the English concern themselves with "just conquest." Instead, they either claimed that the land was vacant, as the Pilgrim Fathers did in Plymouth Colony, or declared the land forfeit, as the Anglicans did after 1622 in Virginia. The early English attitude in the Americas, therefore, was one of Puritan parochialism rather than Catholic cosmopolitanism. Nevertheless, as time passed, variations developed in this English attitude, not just between New England, which did not depend on slavery, and Virginia, which did, but also between Virginia and Barbados —although both were plantation colonies.

All the European colonies in the New World found it uniformly necessary to import African slaves to do their labor both in their homes and in the fields. Almost all Europeans generally believed that slavery was compatible with their religion and their society. Individual critics such as Bartolomé de las Casas and the Abbé Raynal were always present, and sometimes large groups had fleeting misgivings. The penal settlement of Georgia thought slavery was not a good thing, but that thought quickly passed. By 1660 the plantation society had begun to appear at various places in the Americas, and this slowly altered the relations between masters and slaves everywhere. Slavery became more than an economic asset or an organizational convenience; it became a part of the values of the society, a part of the social mores.

Slave Societies in the New World

How do we compare slave societies in the New World? Before we can do this, we must know what conditions were typical for any given slave society in any area of America. This is not an easy task. The quality of slave life and the conditions of slavery varied considerably throughout the New World. There is no doubt about this assertion, and historians have been debating the variations for a very long time. But while it is easy to arrive at some idea of the general conditions of slavery, it is less easy to determine the general quality of slave life from place to place and from century to century.

Most people who have tried to compare slavery in the Americas have done so according to the imperial systems and national boundaries of the slaveholding groups. This is especially true of North American historians. The general consensus classified slavery along a continuum that had the Anglo-Saxons, that is, the United States and the British Islanders, as the most cruel and inhumane slaveowners, and the Iberians—the Spanish Americans and the Brazilians —as the most humane. And somewhere in the middle fell the French, the Dutch, and the Danes.

These thinkers on slavery and slave societies make useful contributions to our understanding of the subject. The difficulty is that they all use a "rigid" theory to explain a dynamic and changing social phenomenon. Slave societies, like all other societies, were never static. In all slave societies, therefore, there were stages, or even a single stage, when slavery was more important, socially, politically, and economically, than at other times. Barbados was a mature slave society in 1660; but by 1780 slavery had been in decline, and by 1838 it was abolished. The most important phase of slavery in the United States came only after the abolition of the English transatlantic slave trade in 1808. The majority of the slaves in the United States, therefore, were produced locally, not imported from Africa, which was a truly American phenomenon. About 75 percent of all Cuban slaves came during the nineteenth century, at a time when very few countries still engaged in slavery and the slave trade. Brazil, on the other hand, was a consistently high importer of slaves between the sixteenth and the nineteenth centuries.

One significant problem in comparing and categorizing American slave societies is simply timing. Except for Brazil, there was no uniform participation in the slave trade and slavery. Some countries were early starters, others late starters; some remained always important participants, such as Brazil or Jamaica, while Peru and Ecuador were quite unimportant. Cuba, Trinidad, and Venezuela developed significant slave components only during the very last days of slavery in the Americas.

Another problem is the internal diversity of slave societies. Within each society, slaves did a very wide variety of work. The view held by the society as a whole seems to be related to the numbers and jobs that they did. In any case, the conditions of slave life and the general attitudes toward slavery by the free society sprung from the role of slavery.

Two patterns existed in American slaveholding societies. One was the individual-ownership pattern, in which a master had from one to four slaves. These slaves were usually domestic slaves, or personal assistants in towns, but also included slaves who were engaged in such activities as piracy, ranching, and fishing. The other was the group-ownership pattern, where the masters owned slaves in large numbers for plantation or mining work.

Individually owned slaves had advantages and opportunities that group-owned slaves lacked. The most important aspect of the individual-ownership pattern was the absence of coercion and regimentation in their occupations. This is especially true of the largest group of such slaves, the urban slaves. Urban slaves had a wide range of social and sexual contacts with fellow slaves, with the free nonwhite community, and with the free white community. Urban slaves had some social and legal resources—the intervention of the minister or employer in the southern United States; or the priest and government-appointed "Protector of Slave Rights" in Cuba during the nineteenth century—which for all practical purposes did not exist for the nonurban slaves.

Most writers on slavery generally concede that urban slaves, regardless of their occupations, established an understanding and a relationship with free society—and with their masters—which was not duplicated elsewhere. Having access to more money, urban slaves fed and dressed themselves better and certainly enjoyed themselves more, drinking, dancing, and entertaining openly where it was legal, or clandestinely where it was not. Since the day-to-day life of these slaves was less regimented than in the mines and on the plantations, these slaves tended to escape from slavery either through self-purchase or outright desertion. Moreover, their established connections with the free community also facilitated their way out of slavery.

With greater mobility, a greater range of contacts, and probably a greater degree of literacy, urban slaves tended to be more aware of their individual rights. The physical restraints and punishment of the rural areas had no place in the towns. Masters with troublesome slaves sent them off to the country or sold them.

Slaveholders disliked the urban setting for slaves. A Louisiana planter declared during the nineteenth century that slavery did not thrive "when transplanted to the cities," for the slaves became "corrupted," "dissipated," and "acquire the worst habits." Perhaps for this reason the general conditions and the number of urban slaves tended to decrease in both Cuba and the United States during the nineteenth century. Between 1820 and 1860, the percentage of urban slaves in the southern states fell from 22 percent to 10 percent. Between 1855 and 1870 the number of urban slaves decreased by nearly 20,000 in Cuba. Brazil had nearly four times as many rural slaves as there were urban and domestic. The urban-industrial complex was disastrous to slavery.

Rural domestic slaves also tended to share the opportunities of the urban slaves. In parts of the South, Cuba, St. Domingue, Martinique, Guadeloupe, Venezuela, and Brazil, the ostentatious luxury of the *Casa Grande* (the Great House), as the

Brazilian Gilberto Freyre called it, required a number of domestic servants. And just as in the urban setting, these slaves tended to have a broader and freer system of social relations. Many were literate—deliberately taught by their masters or surrepticiously self-instructed. A number tended to be emancipated as a reward for faithful service, and some females derived special favors from the close relationship they developed with white males. But while domestic slavery extended the cosmopolitanism of the slave, it hardly facilitated any greater reconciliation to the system. Indeed, rural domestic slaves often were key figures in slave revolts; and the most successful slave rebel, Toussaint L'Ouverture, the "Father of Haiti" (even though he did not declare its independence), came from the ranks of the privileged domestics.

Slaves who were engaged in such activities as piracy, cattle herding, or fishing were virtually free men. But piracy, cattle herding, and fishing did not employ a large number of slaves anywhere, and so these occupations did not significantly affect the general nature of slavery in any particular country.

The worst conditions by far existed for group-held slaves in mines, in small, poor, rural communities, and on plantations. Slaves on plantations and in mines formed a class unto themselves. For not only were the physical requirements of the mines and plantations more demanding, but the daily routine of the slaves was far more circumscribed. Part of the reason for this regimentation of slavery on plantation, in mines, and in the rural areas generally came from the method of production. Slaves did the repetitious, boring, and unskilled jobs. But their jobs had to fit into certain production deadlines, whether they were picking cotton, casing tobacco, or producing sugar. In any case, profit depended on a crude efficiency, and efficiency depended on careful organization and coordination.

Another reason for regimenting the lives of these slaves was for better control. Rural slaveholders usually had many more slaves than urban slaveholders. In the American South, for example, urban slaveowners, averaged less than 5 slaves. Indeed, in 1860 nearly 60 percent of all slaveowners had less than 5 slaves each. In plantation-tidewater Virginia the median holdings were between 24 and 28. The differences are even apparent on an island like Cuba, which had a tradition of urban living. The Cuban census for 1857 had an overall island ratio of 1 slaveowner to 8 slaves. In the towns, however, the mean holding was roughly 3 slaves per owner, while the rural owners had a mean of 12 slaves. The 483 largest Cuban slaveholders averaged 197 slaves each. This pattern of slaveholding in Cuba and the United States was also similar to that in Brazil.

The rural slaves lacked the numerous avenues of mobility that their urban counterparts enjoyed. But this did not mean that they were entirely without some degree of mobility. A male rural slave with special skills could be sent off to work in the towns or in some industrial enterprise. Such a slave could then accumulate sufficient money to purchase his freedom. Likewise, an attractive female slave could win the affection of her master and be promoted to domestic service in the Great House. With some luck she might even be granted her freedom on the deathbed of her master, for the practice of manumission in last wills was not infrequent throughout the slave societies of the Americas.

THE EFFECT OF SLAVERY ON RACE RELATIONS

Slavery became a fundamental part of the American exploitation colony with its various plantations. It began as a method of labor organization and land control. But within a short time it assumed social and economic importance. In legal and customary terms, the relations between masters and slaves became increasingly more defined. For slaves were both rational beings as well as property. As rational beings they required police-control measures; as personal property they were subject to the treatment given to chattel. The American slave and the American white, therefore, had to work out a new type of relation in the Americas other than the one that they had formulated along the African coast. This new master-slave relation happened all across the imperial boundaries in the Americas—in English America, Spanish America, French America, Portuguese America, and Dutch America.

The plantation socioeconomic complex first developed in Brazil in the sixteenth century, sometime between 1540 and 1580—about forty years after Brazil was discovered and about 100 years before plantations began elsewhere. The plantation began as the medium of providing Europe with tropical staples that were in short supply but great demand: sugar from sugar cane, tobacco (which was an American contribution to European society), cotton, indigo, rice,and anil. From the very outset it was designed as a system in which Europeans came to organize the production and export, while doing as little of the work themselves as possible. At first the poor and the unfortunate of Europe were coerced into going to work in the tropics or were transported for a variety of petty misdemeanors that scarcely deserved attention. Criminals and poor aspiring emigrants were indentured to a fixed period of service overseas. But by the middle of the sixteenth century it was clear that Europe could not supply the required laborers for the American plantations. The planters reorganized the native American Indians and imported Africans. By the eighteenth century, slavery had become synonymous with the Indians and the Africans, although more with the Africans than the Indians.

The exact details of the establishment of the plantation society varied slightly from place to place in the Americas. But everywhere the basic ingredients became imported African labor and European capital and managerial skills. The white community formed a permanent settler society in the southern United States, Cuba, Venezuela, and Brazil. In the Antilles the white society was a largely transient group, with its values, inclinations, and desires focused on the metropolis. These whites saw the tropics as areas to be exploited, where plantations could be established. The plantation slave societies of America, especially the sugar plantation societies, did not lend themselves to a great degree of variety or flexibility. The society was sharply divided along racial lines, with three internally subdivided groups of slaves, free people of color, and free whites. Despite the mutual hostility of the races, it was possible for some persons to cross the racial barriers. Legal restrictions did not prevent some people with African blood to "pass as white" in the United States. Passing was even easier outside the United States of America. Slave society in the United States, however, did become more polarized by its early tendency to categorize people rigidly as white or black and to establish sharp legal distinctions between the races. Thus the rigidity and inflexibility of the system of categorization during slavery may have been crucial in the formation of race relations and attitudes after slavery. For the economic role and the social and legal recognition of each group greatly affected their attitudes toward the slave system and their society. This seemed especially true for the intermediate, racially mixed group that was ambiguously juxtaposed between free and slave. These were the free nonwhite persons, black or mulatto, born in Africa or the Americas, and sometimes the biological offspring of an African and a European.

THE POSITION OF THE FREE PERSON OF COLOR

In the United States the number of free Afro-Americans reached nearly half a million by the end of slavery, or about 12 percent of the entire population of African descent. Most of these free Afro-Americans lived in the slave states, particularly Louisiana, North Carolina, Virginia, and Maryland. The attractive facilities of the towns and the general hostility to the black and mulatto population forced the free persons of color away from the countryside. In Maryland, for example, more than 25,000 of the slightly less than 84,000 free blacks lived in the city of Baltimore. In Louisiana, more than 10,000 of the approximate 13,000 free Afro-Americans lived in New Orleans. Similarly, other towns such as Mobile, Vicksburg, Natchez, and Memphis attracted substantial numbers of free blacks. In the towns they performed a variety of skills, often in competition with the poor whites.

A surprisingly large number of free black families remained in the rural areas, farming the land, and, despite the formidable obstacles, sometimes even owning slaves and being successful planters. A large majority, however, were forced by their society to survive at a mere subsistence level, whether they practiced some skill or trade or worked for themselves or part-time for others. Nevertheless, the historical record will probably show that the black population was just as ambitious and industrious as the rest of the population—they just had greater legal and political disabilities that depressed their social conditions.

Until the Civil War in the United States, the position of the free colored population tended to worsen gradually, although great differences existed from place to place. Economic opportunities seemed to have been getting better in eastern Virginia and Maryland at about the same time that they deteriorated in Charleston and New Orleans. By the 1850's many states were attempting to impose slavery on the free colored population, although only a few succeeded. And everywhere the handicaps increased for the free colored population to own property.

The attempts to demote the free black population and undermine its political and economic position resulted from the anomaly of this group in the two-caste slave society that prevailed in the southern United States. The society was perplexed by this group, which was neither part of the slave forces nor the free community, and tried to clarify the position by eliminating this group. The free black population, however, tried to accommodate itself to the society and stubbornly refused to be obliterated.

The progressive social decline of the black population continued after the Civil War, despite the unfounded optimism of Reconstruction. Southern society had been convinced that slavery was a good thing. For the great majority of poor whites who could not afford to own slaves, slavery provided a psychological lift, the feeling of a superior position. Slavery, in other words, established a pattern of race relations that was accepted in the South. Abolition upset the pattern by destroying the relations between blacks and whites. The subsequent history of segregation and discrimination in the South indicates that a desire existed on the part of the whites to reimpose the previous racial duality of southern society.

Elsewhere in the Americas the free colored population did not suffer the same rigid exclusion of the southern United States. Perhaps the reason lies with the general acceptance of the three-tiered society rather than a dual-strata society. Two observations can be made about the free colored population outside the United States of America. The first is that some sort of distinction was made between all the white people and the free people of color. The second is that during periods of scarce labor, the freedom of this group became imperiled—as it was in Spanish Cuba during the nineteenth century and Dutch Surinam from the early eighteenth century until 1850.

In the British West Indies, just as in the British North American colonies before 1776, freedmen and their descendants were not allowed the full rights of citizenship. The disabilities varied from island to island as the regulations were made by the local legislatures. Most discriminatory laws came in the eighteenth century when the plantation society was at its zenith. In general they tended to restrict ownership of property and to limit the right to inheritance and to deny judicial rights, the right to vote, and the right to sit in local assemblies.

The Jamaica laws, though designed to fit the peculiarities of that colony, represented the general pattern by which this part of the population suffered subordination and exclusion. Free colored people first lost the right to employment in any public office; two years later, in 1713, they were barred from serving in any supervisory position on estates. In 1732 they lost the right to vote. In 1761 they were forbidden to purchase land valued more than 2,000 Jamaican Pounds (about £1,200 sterling). At the same time, they could not receive any inheritance exceeding £2,000 sterling unless the Assembly passed a private bill that would make an exception in every individual case.

The change for the free colored population came just after the loss of the North American colonies, and significantly, as the plantation system began its rapid decline. The free colored population began to regain their civil rights. Interestingly enough, these rights were regained while the black population in the United States experienced its sharpest reversals. Obviously, the nonsettler whites of the English Caribbean did not feel sufficiently strong about the island society to interpret the change as a fundamental threat to their way of life. The few who did so were in no position to do anything about it. In 1796 the free colored person in the British West Indies could give evidence in a court of law for the first time. In 1813 such evidence was admitted against a white person—a very significant achievement in the slave society. By 1832, the eve of the abolition of slavery by the British Parliament, all the British West Indies had removed the civil disabilities of the free colored community. The society, therefore, became divided not according to race and color but by status of free and slave.

The admission of the free colored community to the civil equality of the white stratum of the society was to have momentous legal and political consequences for the British Caribbean. Since the racial barrier had already been broken down for the free colored community, all the remaining black persons became equal citizens with the whites after the abolition of slavery in 1838. The Caribbean islands, therefore, provided the prospect of a majority black population, sharing equally (at least in theory) the status of their former masters. This black population quickly moved to establish itself as peasant proprietors, artisans, petty bureaucrats, and professional people. Economic and political power eluded them for more than a century afterwards, but at least they did not have the added psychological scars of a minority population in a hostile environment.

Throughout the French Antilles, the rights of all freedmen were guaranteed by the *Code Noir,* or general imperial slave regulations passed by Louis XIV in 1685. Notwithstanding, the French colonial planters passed a series of ordinances in their local legislative councils (the *Conseils Souverains,* a weaker replica of the Planters Assemblies in the English Antilles), which reduced the half-castes, or mulattoes, to the status of second-class citizens. The French Revolution brought the awareness of racial and class equality to the islands. By 1805, St. Domingue, the pride of the French Empire, had become the first black republic in the Western Hemisphere—and the second independent state in the New World. In Martinique and Guadeloupe, the plantation status quo was restored by Louis XVIII in 1815, largely owing to the greater proportion of white settlers and the small size of the islands, which made them vulnerable to English naval might.

The legal status of the free people of color in Brazil was identical to that of a free person of any other color. Group distinctions, however, prevailed. Under the Portuguese empire these distinctions took the form of privileges given to the large landowners, the clergy, the military, and the members of Portuguese nobility. The rest of the population, including the free Afro-Brazilian, had no privileges beyond the distinction that they were not slaves. Perhaps the most significant observation about the Brazilian society was that class and caste were important when economic distinctions were not sharp. On the other hand, the small economic differences probably resulted in less racial friction between the various free groups. In Brazil, however, the free colored population included people of African, European, and American Indian ancestry. But the group was never strictly defined in legal terms, and occasionally a colored person could rise through the ranks and become a member of the privileged group. In order to do this, all he needed was a light skin color and a great deal of money. Until today, Brazilians claim that "money whitens."

The Spanish colonial system, just like that of the Portuguese, divided itself along lines of privilege. Nonwhites were prohibited from wearing certain clothes and jewels and even from practicing certain occupations reserved for the white people. But the divisions allowed some mobility, and occasionally a colored person would buy his way into the white group, thus legally and practically enjoying all the privileges of that position. And as in Brazil, a lot of money and a fairly light skin color were prerequisites that facilitated the transition.

The situation in the Netherlands Antilles approximated that of the British West Indies. Persons of color who had a great deal of "European blood," or were "whiter," enjoyed certain privileges over the other free coloreds. They were called *mesties* and identified as burghers or citizens. Nevertheless, class, race, and color were significant elements in Dutch colonial society; however, the situation may have varied between the urbanized and commercial Curaçao and the predominantly plantation Surinam.

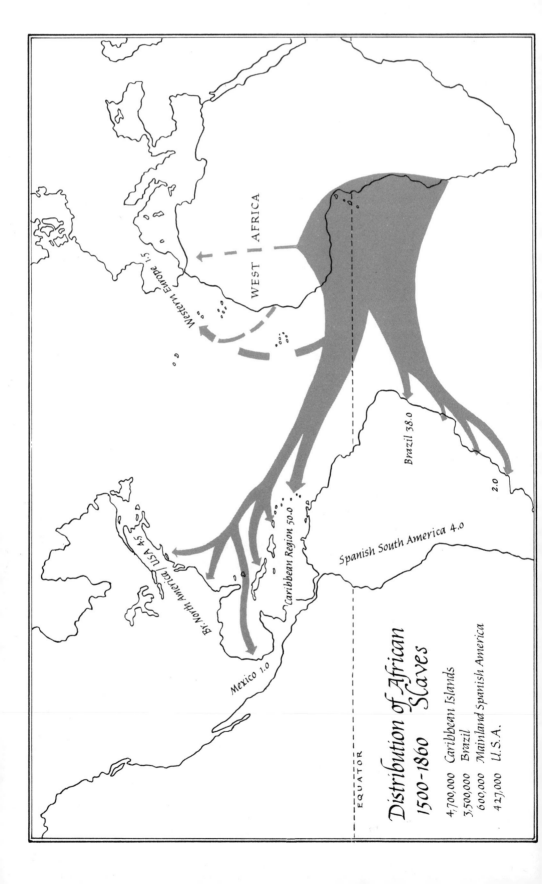

WEST AFRICA

Western Europe 1.5

Brazil 38.0

2.0

Spanish South America 4.0

Caribbean Region 50.0

Br. North America / U.S.A. 4.5

Mexico 1.0

EQUATOR

Distribution of African Slaves
1500 – 1860

4,700,000   Caribbean Islands
3,500,000   Brazil
600,000   Mainland Spanish America
427,000   U.S.A.

SETTLER VERSUS NONSETTLER AMERICA

The role and treatment of the free colored community reflect the degree to which the slave society was part of a European settlement colony. Variations in the social development between the United States and other parts of the Americas, as well as within the United States, also resulted from this historical fact.

Unlike the other slave societies, the South was a settler society. People went there to make a fortune, produce a family, and spend their lives. The white people outnumbered the slaves and other nonwhites. But what is more, these people did not, after 1776, represent offshoots of another society, as in Cuba or Jamaica or Brazil. As an independent and cohesive entity, the Southerners fashioned their own world view. In their view of the world, slavery formed an integral part of the social system. Men who did not, or could not, afford to have slaves thought the slaveowners to be their social superiors. And perhaps because they themselves aspired to that position, they supported the system. The majority of the Southern whites who fought to perpetuate the system of slavery during the Civil War did not themselves own slaves.

As a predominantly settler society, the plantation, though necessary, became an appendage, not the *raison d'être* as in the Caribbean and Brazil. The decline of the plantation economy did not represent the disintegration of their society. When Southerners such as George Fitzhugh attacked the capitalist Northerners, they feared less the economic power of their neighbors than the threat to their way of life implicit in industrial capitalism. What seemed to bother them most of all was the fact that capitalism accepted in principle the equality of all men—or at least ranked men according to their success in acquiring material things. The Southern view was a racist one: The poor, white pauper was "superior" to the wealthy black planter.

There was also a sexual angle involved. As a settler society the South had more white women. White young men might pursue illicit sexual relations with black women—and the great number of mulattoes in the South testify to that—but they married white women. This often precluded the recognition of their half-caste offspring, who legally became both slaves and "black." On the other hand, in the Caribbean and Brazil, the presence of a third stratum (and the short supply of white women) facilitated manumission, or granting of liberty to the free half-castes. They did not become a threat to the social system.

SLAVE MORTALITY AND AFRO-AMERICAN POPULATION DISTRIBUTION

TABLE 2 *Slavery and the Growth of the Afro-American Population, 1500–1890*

Area	Total slaves imported	Percentage of the slave trade	Afro-Am. population (year)	Percentage local population
U.S.A.	427,000	4.5	4,500,000 (1860)	7.0
Caribbean Islands	4,700,000	43.0	2,000,000 (1880)	60.0
Mainland Sp. America	600,000	6.0	600,000 (1810)	3.5
Brazil	3,500,000	38.0	4,000,000 (1890)	33.0

The U.S. South was the only part of America to have a self-reproducing slave population. This phenomenon had important bearings on slavery throughout the Americas. Only in the United States did the slave population have a natural increase compared to the free population. This healthy natural increase suggests a contrast between the United States and the rest of the American hemisphere. Maybe the diet of the North Americans was radically different, perhaps better. Or the structure of North American slavery, especially the family and sexual relations, was more conducive. Historians have not yet explored and explained these differences.

The contrasting figures (provided in Table 2) between slave populations and Afro-American populations surviving slavery illustrate the high mortality rate of slaves. The North American colonies, plus Florida and Louisiana, imported approximately 427,000 African slaves during the entire period of the transatlantic trade. At the time of the Civil War, the slave population alone had reached nearly 4 million. The Afro-American population, both slave and free, was approximately 4.5 million in 1860.

Elsewhere, the slave population at the end of slavery was considerably less than the total number of imported Africans. Brazilian planters brought more than 3.5 million slaves to Brazil between 1500 and 1850. The slave population at the time of emancipation in 1888 was slightly more than 700,000, with an additional 1.3 million freedmen. In 1890 the black population was just above 2 million—although the mulatto population was more than twice that number.

Jamaica imported a net total of more than 600,000 Africans during the eighteenth century. Despite births, the population at the end of the century was a little more than 300,000—a figure that declined even further before the abolition of slavery in 1838. The French colony of St. Domingue imported more than 800,000 slaves during the eighteenth century. In 1790, on the eve of the great rebellion, the slave population was slightly more than 480,000. During the nineteenth century Cuba imported more than 600,000 slaves, yet less than 200,000 were emancipated in 1886. Although the Caribbean islands imported nearly 5 million slaves, in 1880 the black population slightly exceeded 2 million.

In the United States the slave population increased at an average rate of about 3 percent per year during the nineteenth century. In the other parts of the hemisphere the slave population tended to show an absolute decline of between 2 percent and 4 percent per annum. The causes of these differences are numerous and complex. Diet, diseases, and sexual imbalance were important, along with the inhibiting restraints and exhaustive demands of a brutal system based on coercion and regimentation. In the United States slave-breeding was an economic enterprise. Elsewhere, the goals of plantation production excluded this possibility. There is no evidence that slaveowners were more callous in any one place than in another.

TABLE 3   *Percentages of Slave Importations, Afro-American Population, and Racial Mixture in 1950*

Region	Percentage of the total American slave trade	Percentage of total Afro-Americans in 1950	Percentage of mixed population in 1950
Brazil	38.0	37.0	26.0
U.S.A.	4.5	31.0	5.0
Cuba	7.0	3.0	15.0
Br. Caribbean	17.0	8.0	20.0
Haiti	9.0	6.0	10.0

It is interesting to compare the distribution pattern of the present Afro-American population throughout the Americas. (See Table 3.) Except for Brazil, there is little relation between the proportion of the Africans imported and the proportion of the Afro-American population in the middle of the twentieth century. In the United States the Afro-American population has increased tremendously from a low slave base. In the Caribbean, and some other parts of plantation America, the Afro-American population is proporcionately far less than the number of slaves imported.

Nevertheless, the degree of racial mixing in the United States is less than elsewhere. What does this mean? It means that while the conditions for survival were better in the United States than elsewhere, the society was more sharply divided along racial lines. Even more important, the larger Afro-American population still remained a minority population in the United States.

Summary

Almost all the ancestors of the present Afro-American population came to the Americas as slaves. Before the nineteenth century more Africans than Europeans came to the New World, but they held a subordinate position in the new societies. This did not change after the abolition of slavery.

The heritage of slavery was a handicap because most free white people did not regard slaves or ex-slaves as equal human beings.

A dual pattern of slavery existed in the Americas. One pattern was the large-scale ownership of slaves, usually on plantations producing crops for export. The other was the ownership of small numbers, usually in the household. The two patterns then overlapped in areas of settler America and nonsettler America. Local conditions exerted the greatest influences on the conditions of slaves.

The Afro-American population distribution was only the most obvious legacy of slavery. More general but harder to document and explain were the varying attitudes toward race and slavery. These attitudes developed before the profiles of the American societies were drawn, for each group has the inherent characteristic of defining its attitudes and relations to every other group. But the geographical, social, political, and economic conditions produced varying configurations of the same theme. We shall turn our attention to the genesis of these attitudes in the next chapter.

Chapter 3

American Attitudes Toward Race and Slavery Before the Twentieth Century

WHITE AMERICAN ATTITUDES toward race and slavery underwent a constant change over the years. These attitudes derived partly from the Christian tradition of Europe but reflected the varying local experiences of slavery. They can be traced along the patterns of settlement, lines of color, or degree of racial mixture in the different societies. The process is complex because the societies themselves were fluid, and outside influences always played a role in the definition of attitudes. By the middle of the nineteenth century, however, the distinction between the United States of America and the rest of the hemisphere had become quite clear, that is, the distinction between settler and nonsettler America.

Race, Color, and the Christian Tradition

Attitudes toward race and attitudes toward slavery are not necessarily the same. To begin with, race is a complex and ill-defined term that has many connotations. It is also a word that has undergone constant semantic change. Race is a form of identification. Initially it began as a part of the ever expanding circles of contact and differentiation that characterize society from the family to the national group. Distinctions originate within the family. The process starts with an awareness of self, of parents, of brothers and sisters and leads through members of the extended family, friends, members of the village, and onwards and outwards. The awareness of race began at the level of political divisions. Englishmen before the fifteenth and sixteenth centuries thought of themselves as a race distinct from the Spanish and Portuguese (whom they called "Dons" and "Portingals") and other Europeans. And they perhaps thought of themselves as a separate race from the Irish and the Scots.

As Europeans pushed ever farther into the wider world, and as they began to realize the diversity of the colors and conditions of man and society, they changed their notions of race. Race took on characteristics of color. All Europeans were "white," Africans were "black," Asians were "yellow," and American Indians were "red" or "copper colored." The realization that all Europeans had enough in common to form a group and that non-Europeans constituted an outgroup was a very important development in the evolution of attitudes toward race. For after that the color element in race replaced the previous distinctions of "Christian" and "infidel" or "citizen" and "barbarian," which had existed among men.

The evolution of a concept of race did not stop with the awareness of the color ingredient. It continued through time, reflecting the increased complexity of society and the rise of scientific knowledge. During the nineteenth century many persons were convinced that some races were naturally superior to others; and even though Charles Darwin himself was skeptical, they derived their support from his *Origins of Species*, published in 1859. Darwin's theory of evolution came on the heels of more than 200 years of speculation on the nature of man and society. During the eighteenth century one of the most popular beliefs of educated men was the "Principle of Plenitude," which claimed that all the animals of the world were fitted hierarchically along a Great Chain of

Being, "from man down to the smallest reptile, whose existence can be discovered only by the microscope."

Once intellectuals, especially scientists, began to talk about divisions and classifications of men, they automatically began to make qualitative distinctions among the men they classified. But there were no proper ways for an accurate qualitative grouping of mankind, whereby some men may be deemed "higher" or "better" than others. The basis for this qualitative division, therefore, came from personal and subjective impressions. Europeans were more familiar with themselves and their culture. They were more or less satisfied, and this satisfaction coupled with their ignorance and fear of other cultures resulted in their mental subordination of the rest.

The inclination to despise the unfamiliar is characteristic of all groups. The Europeans held no monopoly in this. Chinese, Japanese, Turks, and Africans had similar views of people foreign to their region. What made the European attitude different from the others was their power position in world affairs beginning about the late sixteenth century. By the late nineteenth century the Europeans had achieved a clear dominance over the nonindustrialized, non-European world. The standards for classifying the people of the world became, for better or worse, the standards of the Europeans.

Long before the Europeans had established their supremacy in international politics, economics, and technology, however, they had formed ideas about race in general and Africans in particular. The Europeans had a view of the world that gave them the central and dominant position and other people the peripheral and subordinate position. Their attitude toward the people of African origin and descent reflected both their internal class distinctions and relations as well as the historical experience of African slavery.

As early as the middle of the sixteenth century, Juan Ginés de Sepúlveda had smeared the benign corporatist traditions of St. Thomas Aquinas and Aristotle with racism. For Sepúlveda argued that some men were naturally superior to others because they could reason better than the others. From this basic premise he derived that some races of men were superior to others—a logical sequence without biological support. Some races, therefore, should rule over the others, which became their slaves. What Sepúlveda had done was to fashion a world in which "natural slaves" existed. He had no doubt that the Spaniards of the sixteenth century were the best of the "natural superiors," whereas the American Indians and Africans were only fit to be slaves.

Sepúlveda's argument did not have great appeal at the time. The Spanish monarch, Charles V, preferred the humanitarian appeal of Bartolomé de las Casas. Moreover, by the time that Sepúlveda had announced his racist ideology, the Pope had already declared the Americans to be rational men, equal to the Spanish in their ability for spiritual preparation for the kingdom of heaven.

But there was another disturbing implication of the identity of race and slavery that Sepúlveda made. He had gone beyond the teachings of St. Thomas Aquinas and suggested that might equaled right. Of course, this was not explicit in his argument—he was too much a man of his times for that. The sixteenth century was still a highly religious age, and Roman Catholics tried hard to avoid the sins of pride and greed, which their American conquests suggested. Thomas Aquinas posited a hierarchy in which subordination had a purpose in nature and in which the strong had a moral duty to protect the weak. Sepúlveda made the strong the rulers as well as the masters. If the battle was lost in the sixteenth century, the war was eventually won by the eighteenth century when the ideas of racism began to flower.

It would be as serious an error to think that there was one single attitude held by all white people toward the Africans, just as it was farcical to think that all Africans were similar. We have already made reference to the English attitude and the Iberian attitude. We ought constantly to bear in mind that in every European country different people had varying degrees of awareness of and physical and psychological responses to the African. The English sailor or planter or traveler had a much clearer vision of the African than the rest of their compatriots who had only seen pictures of an African, which were often grotesquely exaggerated. Similarly, the Por-

tuguese of the Algarve or the Spanish of Huelva, Seville, or
Malaga had far greater contact with Africans than Spaniards
from Pamplona or San Sebastian. Nevertheless, all Europeans of a given period shared a certain tradition and formed
a general attitude to which they adhered to a greater or lesser
degree. By the seventeenth century slavery and colonialism
had accentuated the cultural differences between Europeans
and non-Europeans. Ever afterwards, European technological superiority reinforced their ethnocentricity. To be non-
European was to be "inferior."

Winthrop D. Jordan has shown in his book, *White over
Black, American Attitudes to the Negro, 1550–1812,* that
Europeans in general and Englishmen in particular were adversely predisposed toward all nonwhite people. In other
words, without being aware of it, European white people
feared and hated people who were not like themselves. In
certain social situations, such as the plantation society or the
South African frontier, this subconscious feeling became a
part of their conscious action.

Christian color symbolism, with its standard images of
black sin and white goodness, perpetuated the low esteem of
black people. Since European social attitudes developed from
a predominantly religious base, European relations with
non-Europeans reflected this sensitivity about color. Even
when Europeans have been no longer active advocates of
Christianity, the traditional attitudes of color have neither
been diluted nor dissolved. Instead, changing conditions,
such as the large-scale immigration of nonwhites, Indians,
Africans, and West Indians into Britain, tend to produce a
secular, often virulent racism. This racism is the product
of color prejudice.

Obviously, racial hostility was not the singular result of
Christianity. Economic and sexual situations also produced
racial strife. But the Christian tradition provided a rich variety of color symbolisms that later became attached to racial
groupings. The sharpest dichotomy in Christian thought was
between good and evil, between white and black. According
to Roger Bastide, "whiteness brings to mind the light, ascen-
sion into the bright realm, the immaculateness of virgin snow,

the white dove of the Holy Spirit, and the transparency of limpid air; blackness suggests the infernal streams of the bowels of the earth, the pit of hell, the devil's color."

Other colors fell into place in the heavily prejudicial dichotomy. Blue and gold became associated with white, while yellow and red joined the diabolical black. The Immaculate Virgin of the Roman Catholic Church was always portrayed in white, blue, and gold, while satan was clothed in black with the red flames of hell.

As Europeans moved out into the wider world, the unconscious predispositions to colors were transposed to race. Two simultaneous results followed. In the first place, the Europeans began to be more color conscious, seeing themselves as "whiter" than they were and the other people as "blacker" than they in fact could be. In the second place, the connotations of color that religion had suggested became racial characteristics. Not surprisingly, therefore, the Semitic characteristics of Christ became increasingly more Aryan, or north European. North of the Pyrenees, the pictures of Christ showed a blond, blue-eyed person, who should have been historically quite out of place in the eastern Mediterranean lands. Part of the "whitening" process of Christ was a conscious desire to show the Son of God as far removed from sin as possible. But the fact that this process occurred after contact with non-Europeans revealed a growing color consciousness.

This growing color consciousness affected the relations of non-Europeans. Almost every European traveler after the fifteenth century remarked on the "blackness" of the Africans and the "yellowness" of the Chinese. The Indians of North America were called the "Red Indians." To Europeans black meant sin, yellow meant treason, and red meant hell. Rationalizations developed around these symbols. Christians claimed that a black skin was the punishment God meted out to Cain, who murdered his brother, and Ham, the youngest son of Noah and father of Canaan, who looked at his naked, drunken father and told his brothers about it. According to the account in the Book of Genesis, when Noah became sober, he blessed Shem, the son who had covered him, and declared that "Canaan shall be his servant." Europeans—Christians as well as non-Christians—used this curse to rationalize black slavery in the New World.

Just as rationalization for the exploitation of the African developed from the association of the color of his skin with the traditional Christian symbolism of black so did rationalizations affect European relations with the Asians and the indigenous inhabitants of North America. Early Europeans in Asia—and Westerners ever since—saw Asians as prone to treason because of their color. And as with traits attributed to Africans, this trait was given to all Asians, Chinese or Japanese. The Puritans of New England saw the Indians as children of the devil and beyond the pale of salvation. For by skin color and social and political organization, the Indians represented everything good Calvinists feared: unrestricted liberty, anarchy, and indifference to materialism.

The Importance of Environment

However important and pervasive the traditional Christian attitudes may have been, it was the social environment that gave form and expression to any set of attitudes. One can talk about a general set of ideas that all Christians in the New World might have had, or of the specific ideas which Catholics and Protestants might have shown; yet both sets of ideas cannot be understood outside the context of their social environment and time span.

Iberian Catholics were already a frontier people in contact with Africans when they came to the Americas. Some of the conduct and the ideas of the Iberian Moorish frontier were carried over to the American Indian frontier, especially the traditions of the occupied town, the elite fighting men, and the systems of landholding and government. But the ideals that the Iberians held in the sixteenth century were largely the heritage of their medieval culture. In this medieval culture, knighthood, gallantry, and service were outstanding characteristics, along with the elevation of the white ladies but the abuse of women of lower rank by the feudal lords. While European women of high rank were placed on a pedestal—and perhaps as a result passed their lives in a monotonous, often useless, and repressive existence—the fighting men behaved quite uninhibitedly with the local women. This led to the large mestizo population of Spanish and Portuguese America. But it led to a society in which a dual standard prevailed. Regardless of laws, therefore, people of half-caste or mixed races found a recognized place in the social order. Medieval society was, after all, a stratified society.

Protestant America had a different experience. This variation derived partly because it was Protestant but also partly because by the seventeenth century, the Protestant colonizers came from a different social stratum and represented different ideals. This was true not only of the Anglo-Saxons and the Dutch in the Americas but also of the Dutch Calvinists in southern Africa. The Protestants of that age came from the rising middle classes, to whom industry, thrift, and strict family morals were essential features. The acquisitive zeal that the Protestants displayed was not a part of the African or American Indian heritage. The Protestants, unable to convert the Indian and the Afro-American to their way of life, simply excluded them and then later exploited them as objects of material increase. Africans were not considered among God's elected people.

Strangely enough, the tendency toward secular thought, beginning sometime in the eighteenth century, did nothing to erode the irrational Christian symbolism of color or the fundamental Calvinist tenets of capitalistic zeal. The Enlightenment was, above all, the age of reason, and the nineteenth century the beginning of political democracy. Why, then, did distinctions of race and color persist?

To find a partial answer we must go back to Europe and the ideals of the Europeanized societies overseas. The trend toward secularization in European society accompanied an increase in capitalistic production. The love of pleasure replaced the love for God. An increase in productive power stimulated an increase in consumption, especially as labor and production became more rationally distributed. In the end, the capitalist society became a materialist society: technological, rational, and imperial. These characteristics became the password for civilization.

The social scientists of the nineteenth century saw Africans and Afro-Americans as still clinging to the values that the Europeans had already largely abandoned: the love of the family and tribe, the zeal for religion, and indifference to materialism. To them this meant at best that Africans and Afro-Americans were not as fully developed or civilized as Europeans and at worst that they could never be. The twofold division of human society continued between the European and the non-European, the we and the they, the haves and the have-nots.

In the Americas the attitudes toward race and color reflected both the realities of the local situation and the degree to which the particular American community was an extension of European society. This was generally true for all periods of time. For along with the general outlines of European thought and attitudes went the strong configuration of slavery, the slave society, and their social and demographic heritage.

All too frequently American societies have been divided into masters and slaves, whites and blacks, in a rigid, rather confusing dichotomy. In the days of slavery, some people were not that clearly distinguishable. Today, it is hard to speak of white attitudes and black attitudes—even in the United States where attempts at segregation and discrimination have been taken to their furthest extremes—and have had their greatest effect. Moreover, especially in the Caribbean and elsewhere in Latin America, Afro-Americans certainly demonstrate all the characteristics of industry, thrift, arrogance, and acquisitive zeal attributed to the white Americans. After all, as the majority population, they set the social tone of the Caribbean area.

Settler and Nonsettler America

Both settler and nonsettler American slave society had three basic divisions: white, free persons of color, and slaves. Each group had different general ideas about race and slavery, in just the same way that each group performed different social and economic functions. To a great degree, the body of ideas that each group held reflected the position of that group in the local society. It was generally difficult for a person to move from one group to another—that is, for a person who was free and nonwhite to become free and white. Nevertheless, the degree of social mobility, or the possibilities of any person changing his station of birth, varied considerably from place to place. Moreover, at certain times it was easier than at other times. For this reason, scholars have agreed that the slave society was a rigid society. It is not correct, however, to describe it as a static society since the entire society was constantly undergoing change, even though the relative positions of the three groups remained virtually constant.

For a very long time, white Americans dominated the political, social, and economic structure. Indeed, this was true until the end of slavery, and it continued to be true for most countries in the Americas until the middle of the twentieth century. To a great extent, it is still true of the United States of America today.

The best, though by no means the only, example of settler society was found in the United States. There the white people who came to live thought in terms of permanent settlement. This affected their entire outlook and their relations with the other elements, the free nonwhites and the slaves. For one thing, the groups of whites tended to be larger and more sexually balanced than groups of white transients found in parts of tropical America where the plantations dominated social and economic development.

But in the English North American colonies of the eighteenth century, as later in the United States of America, the white population formed a varying majority, except in South Carolina. While the proportion of whites varied, often considerably from state to state and within each state, the whites outnumbered the nonwhites by more than 2 to 1. At the time of the American Revolution, New England as a whole was about 97 percent white; New York was nearly 86 percent white; New Jersey and Pennsylvania were about 80 percent. From Pennsylvania southward along the Atlantic coastline, the ranks of the whites tended to thin off: Maryland had a white population of less than 70 percent; Virginia had about

60 percent; and South Carolina probably in the vicinity of 40 percent.

Although the proportion and density of the white population varied, and crucial differences developed between the regions, white North Americans saw themselves as a self-conscious community even before 1776. This self-consciousness increased during the nineteenth century and added to the debate and struggle over slavery and the role of the people of African descent in the society. On the one hand, it produced in the North Americans the best-reasoned defense of slavery. On the other hand, it gave to slavery and the post-emancipation North American society a peculiar complexion.

White settler societies existed in Canada and parts of Spanish and Portuguese America, too. In Canada the African made an insignificant impact. And in most parts of settler Ibero-America, the Indian assumed a greater importance than the African. Europeans, at least since the time of Peter Martyr, did not consider the Indians to be "black" and therefore within the realm of their conventional color symbolisms. Perhaps more important for the settler communities outside the United States, the African did not become the important economic asset that characterized the planter societies of the Caribbean and tropical Atlantic lowlands. At any rate, the Spanish Crown failed when it tried to implement its laws prohibiting "contact and communication between Indians and Mulattoes, Negroes and similar races." The society had already begun to move away from ethnic or biological race to a cultural definition of race—the so-called notional race. In other words, the social distinctions were made according to class and culture, not race and color. This development came partly from the greater degree of race mixture in the society. These factors probably facilitated the easy abolition of slavery during the Spanish American civil wars of the early nineteenth century.

The social structure of nonsettler, or plantation America, varied considerably from the general picture of settler America, even though Brazil and Cuba formed a transitional stage. Nonsettler America was a social, economic, and political extension of the European metropolis. It was an artificial

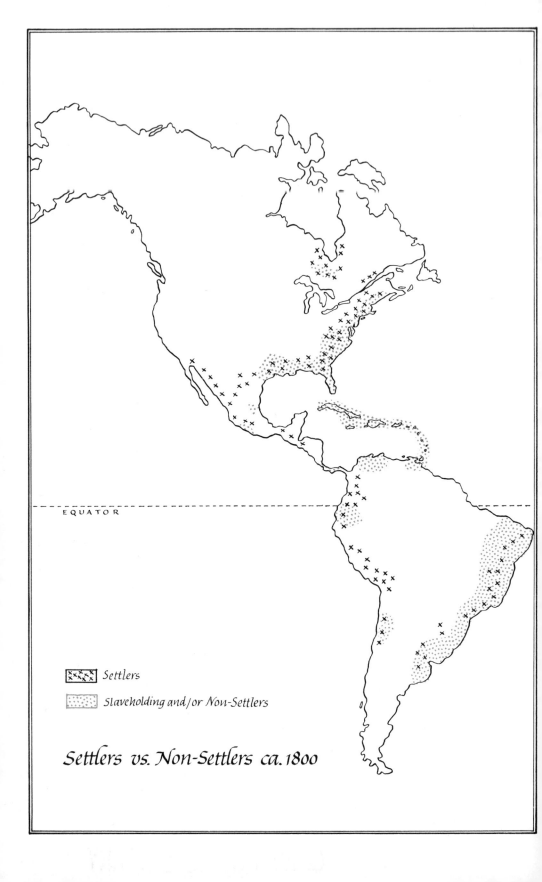

Settlers

Slaveholding and/or Non-Settlers

Settlers vs. Non-Settlers ca. 1800

EQUATOR

complex whose purpose was to supply the mother country with tropical staples. The idea of permanence did not occur to the whites living there, and they behaved like eccentric tourists, or birds of passage.

The white population in the nonsettlement region tended to be a minority of the population. At the top of the society, in terms of status positons, were the whites who either owned estates or held high managerial positions such as overseers and attorneys. These men lived ostentatiously in the great houses. Of course, the owners of estates enjoyed the highest social status. Attorneys, especially those of absentee owners, followed closely. Most owners were, however, absentees, and the attorneys became the highest social class, forming the exclusive cavalry in the militia. Below the attorneys were the overseers, with those able to afford a horse being admitted into the social ranks—and the military ranks—of the attorneys and planters. Lower in social status than estate owners and managers but above any nonwhite group were the merchants, bookkeepers, and other parasitic hangers-on in some British West Indian islands. These hangers-on were there to fulfill the Deficiency Laws, which were designed to keep a sufficient number of white persons on any slave-run estate to boost the morale of the minority and to help in case of riots and rebellions.

In all nonsettler societies, great tensions existed within the managerial white groups, as well as between the white and nonwhite groups. In other words, there were intercaste tensions as well as class tensions in the society. Sometimes these tensions were over social positions, service in the military, or the economic and political relations with the metropolis. Almost always, the problem of slavery crept into discussions and exacerbated the conflict. Because of the dominant position of the white people in the local communities, their problems tended to involve the other groups in society. The tensions thereby generated affected the conduct and relations of the subordinate social strata.

The white ruling caste in both settler and nonsettler America was never unanimously proslavery. From time to time influential individuals spoke out eloquently condemning the institution. Bartolomé de las Casas, although primarily concerned with the plight of the Indians in the early sixteenth century, was the first influential opponent of slavery. In 1573, a Spaniard, Bartolomé de Albornoz, challenged the validity of slavery, but he ran against entrenched economic interests —more powerful than usual since the Spanish Crown was bankrupt—and his treatise was placed on the Index of Forbidden Books.

From time to time, some corporate groups, especially the Church, spoke out not against slavery but in favor of amelioration of the conditions of slave labor. The Church at no time opposed slavery. It actively supported the status quo, it owned slaves, and it vigorously participated in the slave economy. The Jesuits gained a reputation for benevolence and humanitarianism toward their African slaves, yet even they did not oppose the institution of slavery at any time. They were shrewd businessmen who realized such measures further maximized their profits.

During the eighteenth century, when the prosperity of America became more closely tied to slavery and the slave trade, a number of outsiders and visitors to the New World began to question the role and the legality of slavery. These attacks on slavery were directed by individuals rather than any cooperative interests—and many were largely ineffectual. But the attacks on slavery emphasized the divergence that was taking place between the freedom-seeking European society and the frontier society of planters, merchants, and slaves. American slaveowners were forced to justify slavery—something that they had taken for granted prior to that time.

After 1779 the main opponents of slavery were Europeans, like the Abbé Raynal in France and Granville Sharp and William Wilberforce in England. The two most famous proslavery writers of the period, Edward Long and Bryan Edwards, were planters in Jamaica. Both men claimed that Africans derived benefits from slavery. Edwards, however, admitted that the conditions of West Indian slavery needed some improvement. Many planters shared that view, but they declared that slavery was necessary for the economy not only of the region but of the mother country. But even the economic argument lost its appeal during the first part of the nineteenth century when Great Britain and the United States abolished the slave trade and their economies flourished.

The termination of the English slave trade led to greater criticism of slavery and an increasing demand for its abolition. The end of the English trade coincided with the expansion of slavery in parts of settler America—the southern United States, Cuba, and Brazil. There the settlers used more than economic and benevolent arguments to defend the system. Slavery to them was an essential part of their society, and they had great foreboding about any changes. Slaveowners and nonslaveowners were therefore fully prepared to fight to defend their way of life: against an interested North, in the United States; against the Spanish government in Cuba; and against the monarchy in Brazil.

The weakness in defending slavery in nonsettler America is shown in the English colonies. Actually, the position of the British West Indian planters had been untenable. In the first place, as offshoots of English society, they were relatively helpless when crucial decisions about the future of slavery took place in the English Parliament, and in response to English public opinion. In the second place, the West Indian planters had failed to develop any positive arguments in favor of slavery. By 1833 the West Indian plantocracy was economically, politically, and intellectually bankrupt.

The critical phase for the West Indian whites occurred in the 1820's. Humanitarian interest was increasing in Great Britain, and the passage through the House of Commons of the resolutions of George Canning (1823) and Henry Broughan (1826) revealed an unmistakable trend toward the abolition of slavery on the part of the English lawmakers. In the light of this unmistakable trend, the West Indian planters had three basic arguments: that slavery and the colonies were good for the British economy and the English navy; that West Indian slaves were happy, contented, and better off than their African counterparts, or even the English working classes; and, finally, that emancipation would result in the destruction of the society, just as the French slaves had done in St. Domingue in the 1790's.

In the final analysis, the British West Indian planters accepted a part of the £20 million that the parliament voted as compensation money for the loss of their slaves, and everywhere they made adjustment to a new social order in which they held on to political power, shared—albeit grudgingly —the economic power, and watched as a new society came into being. In a sense, the planters had been prepared for the new social order by their intellectual attachment to the mother country. Their terms of reference were those that emanated from England, and they were physically powerless to resist the metropolis.

The plight of the British West Indies was, to a lesser degree, the plight of the French and Danish West Indies. The crucial political decisions were made outside the society. The continental Spanish Americans did not have quite the same problem, but they had had enough of racial inequality during the colonial period to declare unequivocally the freedom and equality of all persons within the state. This did not, of course, make for *de facto* racial equality, but it greatly facilitated the transition from biological race, based on how a person looks (phenotype), to notional race, based on how one behaves. Biological race is essentially genealogical; notional race is essentially a cultural distinction. Unlike the British West Indians, Southerners saw themselves as a fully established society in 1860. While economic and political interests also played a role, most Southerners supported the secession from the Union because they feared the disintegration of the way of life to which they were accustomed. Northern abolitionists may have seen the Civil War as "a moral crusade," but Southerners equally believed in the "morality" of their cause.

The slaveholding classes of Brazil and Cuba lacked the maturity, traditions, and cohesion of the southern United States. These slave societies, therefore, did not produce either the unity or the peculiar slave ideology to defend themselves against the opponents of slavery during the nineteenth century.

By the nineteenth century Brazil had developed two quite dissimilar slaveholding groups. One was the old Northeast, which had engendered the strong patriarchal society so impressively described by Gilberto Freyre in *The Mansions and the Shanties*. There it is possible that the feudalistic pattern of the sugar plantation might have come closest in spirit to the southern United States. But the Northeast had reached its maturity during the eighteenth century, and thereafter it declined economically, socially, and politically. It was also rapidly losing most of its slaves to the South, first to the coffee plantations of the fertile Parahyba Valley of the province of Rio de Janeiro, then further south of São Paulo, beginning in the 1870's.

The new Brazilian slaveholders of the central and southern provinces were less united than those of the old Northeast. They might have shared some of the traditions of the northeastern patriarchs, but essentially they were capitalists, concerned more with an economic system than with a social structure. They felt more strongly about profits than slavery. Moreover, an alliance between slaveowners from the old Northeast and São Paulo did not materialize. As the system became less profitable in the Northeast, the region became more antislavery. In Brazil, therefore, a number of complex factors militated against the establishment of a homogeneous region and world view such as that of the United States. Eventually, the proslavery forces in Brazil used not principles but economics as their main argument—and saw the rug pulled from under their feet. Slavery was not just an economic system.

The Brazil experience found a close parallel in Cuba. Like the Brazilians, most of the new Cuban slaveowners were a new bourgeoisie. Desperately short of manpower, they used slavery as a means of labor organization and as a security against shortages that could cripple the sugar production of a good sugar cane harvest. Unlike the southern states, Cuba was a colony of Spain, subject to political and diplomatic forces against which it had limited control.

The defense of slavery in Cuba, therefore, followed the pattern of the neighboring West Indian islands, emphasizing the value of slavery for the Africans and themselves. But even more than in the neighboring islands, the Cuban arguments reflected the self-interest and immediate socioeconomic conditions of their island. There was absolutely no attempt to justify slavery in the abstract, as was done in the southern United States.

By the time that Cuban slave society matured, it was already far along the way to disintegration. The industrial revolution had its impact on the sugar industry during the latter nineteenth century, requiring skills beyond the competence of the slaves. Skilled labor meant foreign, free, wage-paid, white labor. The mechanization of the sugar industry resulted in the racial integration of the estate labor force, and it blurred the distinctions between "white men's work" and "black men's work," which had traditionally prevailed on the Caribbean plantations.

The Slaves and Slavery

Although most slaves were illiterate, their actions reveal a great deal of their opinions on slavery. Slaveowners often said—even with trembling lips—that their slaves were happy, docile, and tractable. Some later historians have argued that the system of slavery conditioned the slaves to make Pavlovian responses. It is ridiculous to accept these descriptions as valid for all slaves anywhere in the Americas. John Hope Franklin wrote: "It cannot be denied that as old as the institution of slavery was, human beings had not, by the nineteenth century, brought themselves to the point where they could be subjected to it without protest and resistance. Resistance has been found wherever the institution of slavery existed, and Negro slavery in the United States was no exception." *The attitudes of slaves to slavery can be found in the pattern of slave protest and resistance, as well as in the forms or mechanism of accommodation that they developed to the system.*

The objection and resistance of slaves to their conditions covered a wide spectrum. At one end of the spectrum was individual, spontaneous action. Slaves usually vented their anger on animals, killing or maiming them in wanton fashion. Or they killed their masters. Poisoning was a common fear of all slaveowners, from Massachusetts to Montevideo. But the destruction of the master and the master's property was more effective when the slaves mutilated themselves or committed suicide. The removal of their own limbs made them ineffective workers, and laws passed in many places forced a master to support his handicapped slave as long as the slave lived. Suicide was also a major problem everywhere, to the amazement of most slaveowners. In 1807 two cargoes of African slaves in the harbor at Charleston, South Carolina, starved themselves to death. Everywhere stories abounded of slaves who killed themselves by shooting, hanging, knifing, or drowning. In Cuba during the nineteenth century the problem of suicides was so great that it was continually discussed in the Spanish *Cortes* in Madrid. The amazing thing was that the preponderant opinion was that the slaves committed suicide to escape punishment, or because of their lack of a religious conviction based on Christianity. It did not occur to those slaveowners that the massive suicide of their slaves was an eloquent assessment by the slaves of their own conditions. They clearly preferred death to such a life.

Another important piece of evidence was the general affinity to desert their masters, either temporarily or permanently. Slaves who ran away permanently often organized themselves into communities of maroons—a word derived from the Spanish *cimarrón,* meaning "dwellers of the mountain peaks." From 1519 to 1888 the runaway slave was a constant feature of every American society. Slaves ran away from plantations, where they were held in large groups, as well as from towns, where more attractive conditions existed. They ran away at all ages, male and female, alone, in loving pairs, or in conspiratorial groups. The United States had extensive federal and state laws to reduce the practice, but it hardly affected the slaves' unquenchable thirst for freedom. In North Carolina, one woman ran away from her master sixteen times. In Brazil and the British West Indies the maroons were used to foil slave escapes. In Cuba some white people, called *ranchadores,* had the full-time occupation of hunting runaway slaves, both for the sadistic pleasure they derived from seeing their hounds mangle the black bodies as well as for the income they received from the owners.

Some slaves who escaped from their masters lived alone. One such slave was Esteban Montejo, a Cuban runaway slave who published his autobiography in 1968, when he was more than 100 years old. Most slaves, however, formed full communities of varying sizes, where they planted their own crops and behaved like a semiautonomous state within a state. The maroon communities in Jamaica were strong enough to defeat the British and sign two peace treaties in which the British recognized their autonomy for more than 150 years. In Ecuador a group of shipwrecked African slaves intermarried with the local Indians and defied incorporation into the formal structure of the Spanish American empire for more than 300 years. The maroon settlement of Palmares in Brazil was a full-fledged Afro-American state within the Portuguese controlled *Reconcavo*. Palmares once had a peak population of nearly 10,000 inhabitants, drawn from towns and sugar plantations between Bahia and Pernambuco. Formed between 1624 and 1634, the settlement of Palmares came to an end in 1697 only after a long siege by the largest force of Portuguese ever organized in Brazil. Maroon settlements feature prominently in the literature and history of slavery in the Americas. This persistent characteristic belies any suggestion that the American slaves docilely accepted their servitude.

The Free Colored and Slavery

In a similar way, the free colored population rejected and despised slavery. Some free colored persons did own slaves and made a fortune from their participation in slavery, the slave trade, and the slave system. Most free colored persons tried to remove themselves physically and psychologically from slavery. For this reason they moved toward the towns everywhere. In the United States the free colored also moved to the northern states, where they believed their acceptance and opportunities were greater. In the British West Indies the free colored population became lower-echelon bureaucrats, administrators, and professionals—a tradition that extended beyond the days of slavery. Indeed, the black population today dominates the bureaucracy and the professions in such places as Trinidad and Guyana.

During the nineteenth century, while sugar and slavery were still popular and lucrative enterprises in the Spanish Antilles and Brazil, the majority of the free colored community did not participate in this sector of the economy. The vast majority moved outside the coffee and sugar zones and settled in the nonplantation areas, where they toiled on small farms and engaged in small business and services vocations.

Nevertheless, the existence and heritage of slavery did warp the values of the society in general and the nonwhite population in particular. In the Caribbean and continental Spanish America and Brazil, the black population acquired, consciously and unconsciously, the values of the whites. Success and status came in relation to the white minority, not the majority of the population. The African heritage was denigrated and denied. Social values in nonsettler America were essentially European values. The free Afro-American population tried to recognize the virtues of its multiracial, multicultural past and the necessity of improvising for its peculiar conditions. Instead, they mimicked the uncomfortable styles of Europe, assumed a white-oriented bias, and disdained manual labor.

No one has yet studied the full effects of miscegenation and the psychological effects of the ambiguous position of the free colored population in the Caribbean and Latin America. If they seem not to be as adversely affected as their contemporaries in the United States, it is because their history has been different. They have not suffered as much. Social relations in the nonsettler societies were, after all, somewhat more relaxed than in the settler societies. Unlike the situation in the United States, the black population in the Caribbean won recognition in law and custom before the abolition of slavery and became the majority sector of the society. Recognition in law and custom provided a healthy alternative to the maroon settlements as an outlet for the aspirations of the slaves.

The anti-African bias of the days of slavery still prevails, though to a somewhat diminished degree, in the Caribbean today. The models of social organization—complete with class prejudice—and political change remain those inherited from the days of European colonialism. Despite the outstanding influence that West Indians such as Nicolas Guillen, Frantz Fanon, Aimé Cesaire, George Padmore, C. L. R. James, and Marcus Garvey have had on African affairs, there still is little general awareness of African traditions in the West Indies.

African history and literature are neglected in West Indian schools, and the general ignorance of African music and art is amazing. Nevertheless, the African influence prevails in the paintings of some West Indian artists, in religion, in music, and even in the gaiety of local events.

Summary

Settler America used slavery both as a system of labor and an integral pillar of the society. These views were more pronounced in the United States, which was the most mature settler society, than in either Brazil or Cuba where nonsettler influence prevailed. Nonsettlers tended to emphasize the benevolence and economic benefits of slavery. They tended to be less adamant about slavery because they were essentially the offspring of a metropolitan society where the crucial decisions were made.

The attitudes of all white Americans reflected the antiblack bias of Christian Europe. This bias, strongest in settler America, led to racism. But the large numbers of racially mixed persons in Brazil and Cuba reduced or eliminated the polarization that occurred in the United States. Slaves generally hated slavery, even in the United States where birth and custom forced the vast majority to acquiesce. The free colored community tended to be ambivalent, aspiring to the status of the white sector, but handicapped by their skin color. This resulted in a denial of their racial and cultural origins.

While economic considerations were very important, racial composition affected social attitudes. Predominantly black and mestizo societies, such as the Caribbean, Brazil, and Spanish America, show less racial polarization than the United States. Those places emphasize notional race, in which cultural identification is more important than blood or family. On the other hand, the United States defines race according to blood and family. This biological definition of race serves to perpetuate racial polarization, social rigidity, and hierarchial status.

Chapter 4

Group Consciousness and Race Relations in the Twentieth Century

I N THIS CHAPTER we will trace the effect that internal affairs had on the growth of group consciousness and race relations in our two patterns of settler and nonsettler America. For settler America we will look at the United States, Brazil, Cuba, and Puerto Rico. For nonsettler America we will take the English Caribbean, making appropriate references to the French and Dutch Antilles.

The twentieth century, with the massive decline of empire and the vigorous rise of independent states, brought new pressures to bear upon all American societies. The most important change was the emergence of the United States as a world power politically and militarily. This change increased the already strong influence of the United States in the rest of the Americas and blunted—though it did not erase—the distinctions between settler and nonsettler America. The Americas became more or less subordinate to the United States. Military, political, economic, and strategic considerations drew Brazil and the Caribbean region into the United States' sphere of interest. Increased communications, especially radio, television, and teletype, the impact of the two

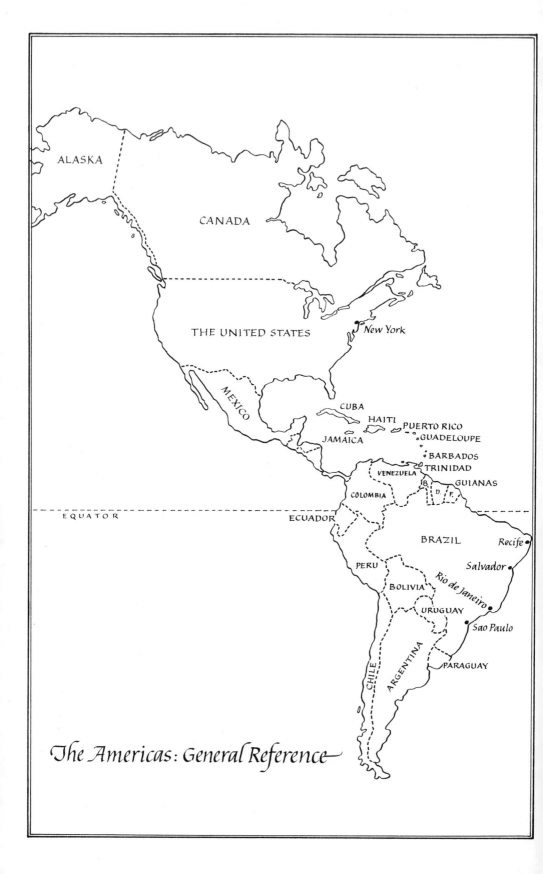

The Americas: General Reference

world wars, and the creation of the United Nations, with its headquarters in New York, all provided a new dimension to the problems of race, locally and internationally.

Despite these changes in the overall world picture, the variations within each country and throughout the Americas continued. Black consciousness and race still played an important role between the North and the South in the United States, in Brazil, and in the Caribbean. Cuba gained its independence, only to be tied economically, first to the United States, and then to the Soviet Union. Puerto Rico formally became an Associated Free State. The predominatly black countries of Barbados, Jamaica, Trinidad and Tobago, and Guyana became independent nations and members of the United Nations. For the first time in their history these new nation-states had to confront the problem of race and identity in a world dominated by white nations. The decisions they made were influenced partly by their history and partly by the circumstances in which they found themselves in the middle of the twentieth century.

The United States

One hundred years after the emancipation of slaves in the United States of America, things had not changed dramatically for the approximately 10 percent of the population who were black. The races still were basically apart. In schools, at work, in buses, in public service, the black population was virtually excluded from meaningful participation in the nation. Despite persistent and responsible advocacy for change by the black people, and despite the periodic, sympathetic response by the federal and some state governments, very little concrete action had been taken anywhere at any level to alleviate the intolerable conditions of the free black population. Even when the federal govenment tried to act, local authorities built a solid wall of obstruction. For example, the 1954 Supreme Court decree to desegregate the schools had been almost disregarded in the South and had only token success in the border states. It was ineffective against the *de facto* residential segregation patterns of the North. On September 22, 1961, the Interstate Commerce Commission ruled that interstate carriers should not use segregated terminals and that passengers on such public interstate carriers could not be segregated by race, color, or creed. Again, however, it was difficult to get some local southern states to comply with the spirit of the law and desegregate intrastate transportation facilities.

The year 1963 began auspiciously enough with the United States Commission on Civil Rights presenting a report, *Freedom to the Free*, to the President. It dealt with the history of civil rights in the United States and emphasized the handicaps of the Afro-American population. Words and aspirations had not been translated into deeds. President Kennedy gave wide publicity to the report, distributing more than 1,000 copies at one social engagement in the White House. He publicly deplored the fact that 100 years after emancipation *bona fide* American citizens had to demonstrate publicly in order to stop at a hotel, eat at a lunch counter, live in the same neighborhood, or attend the same schools on the same terms as other Americans. Vice President Lyndon B. Johnson eloquently articulated the dilemma of America in a speech at Gettysburg. He said: "Until justice is blind, until education is unaware of race, until opportunity is unconcerned with the color of men's skin, emancipation will be a proclamation but not a fact."

Significant changes in race relations came after 1963. That year nearly one quarter of a million people marched on Washington in the torrid heat of summer, singing "We Shall Overcome." The march had the support of every major civil rights, labor, religious, and civic group: the Congress of Racial Equality, the National Association for the Advancement of Colored People, the Southern Christian Leadership Conference, the Students National Co-ordinating Committees, the American Jewish Congress, the National Conference of Catholics for Interracial Justice, the National Council of Churches, the National Urban League, the A.F.L.–C.I.O. Industrial Union Department, and many others. Throughout the decade of the sixties the advocates of reform drew their support from among the young and the idealistic. These were the ones who had responded to the challenge of President

Kennedy to "get the country moving." But the country and Congress remained basically unmoved in its traditional attitudes toward black people and other minority groups until after the assassination of President Kennedy.

The Civil Rights Act of 1964 forbade discrimination and segregation, on the basis of race, color, creed, sex, or age, in housing, education, all public facilities, and elections. It was a fairly far-reaching measure that gave the federal government the power to attack the worst social cancer in the country—segregation and discrimination based on race. The federal government established a number of agencies to implement its new mandate. The Community Relations Service offered to help all individuals and groups having difficulty despite the civil rights bill. An Equal Employment Opportunity Commission became responsible for investigating and resolving inequalities in jobs and job openings. The Office of Education was empowered to assist financially in the desegregation of public schools, thereby gaining the power to withhold funds from those schools that refused to comply with the law. In any case, by the summer of 1964, the passage of the Civil Rights Act, while not an absolute guarantee of equality for the Afro-American, had raised tremendous optimism in all parts and among all people. Thousands of black and white persons, especially from the northern states, traveled throughout the South advising the oppressed poor of their new rights and encouraging them to register to vote in the forthcoming presidential election. The enthusiasm did not last long, and soon the grand illusions were painfully shattered in six years of renewed violence and racial tension between 1964 and 1970.

The sixties were the years of the "black revolution" in the United States, and this revolution was basically political and legislative.

Political disfranchisement created two different societies in the South. With their monopoly of policitcal power, the southern whites had established barriers in schools, housing, family, transportation, and public entertainment. And this pattern gained national sanction by the Supreme Court ruling of 1896, which upheld "separate but equal" segregation as legal.

Political disfranchisement had no legal sanction in the

North. No great lament was heard, however, as the South moved closer to the two separate societies. One reason was the obsession with economic development that took place in the North. Another was probably the conviction that interference with the rights of one state would probably lead to another military conflict between the North and the South. The federal government seemed to agree that the spirit of conciliation was inimical to the direct interference in the affairs of the South, especially after it withdrew federal marshals and election supervisors, in 1894, and granted a general amnesty, in 1898, to all those who had opposed the Union. Yet segregation existed in the North. This was *de facto* rather than *de jure* segregation and was accepted by a majority of all the people. Black and white lived in separate communities, interrelating but not integrating.

The distinct realities of North and South emerged in a curious way. The pace of social change and the increasing divergence between the essentially industrial North and the essentially agrarian South meant that some day, somehow, the vast majority of the black population would be required either in the labor force or the consumer market. Moreover, with the expanding role of the United States in international affairs, the domestic situation in that country would be held up to the scrutiny of the entire world. And these are precisely the factors that came slowly to a climax in the decade of the 1960's when the so-called black revolution took place.

The greater involvement of the United States in international affairs brought a greater awareness of the wider world. Such awareness had always existed in American intellectual life, but only at the higher levels. Scholars, both North and South, were generally well read and quite cognizant of the change in the center of gravity of power politics from Europe to America. After the World War II, increased communications brought ideas and events to the masses. Within the United States the greater degree of communications between people, especially in the towns and cities, brought crowds into situations of confrontation that led to rioting. Most important, however, was the growth in consciousness among the black population, the emergence of what historians then and later called the "new Negro." This new consciousness manifested itself in diverse opposition to the old conditions. They were not going to sit idly by and accept the intimidation of the bigoted whites as their ancestors had done. They fought back with a vengeance in the street battles. Assisted in large measure by the National Association for the Advancement of Colored People, they even fought in the courts to overturn segregated living and other injustices.

The mood of the new Negro found its expression in the Harlem Renaissance of the 1920's, a dynamic literary movement that attracted attention to the social and political plight of the black Americans through the media of writing and drama. The Harlem Renaissance directly or indirectly gave America *Voice of the Negro*, by Robert Kerlin; *Problems of Today*, by Moorfield Storey; the world famous *The Emperor Jones*, by Eugene O'Neill; and *Darker Phases of the South*, by Frank Tannenbaum, the noted Latin Americanist.

The political impact of the Harlem Renaissance was, perhaps, more important than the literary impact. Harlem was in the 1920's what London became in the 1930's and 1940's, Paris in the 1950's, or Dakar in the 1960's: the capital of the race-conscious black man. In poetry, prose, and music, the writers of Harlem attacked every social injustice they could think of—lynchings, segregation, low wages, poor working conditions, and demeaned social status. They were literary craftsmen using their talents in the service of their fellowmen and their country. They were a part of the changing American scene, and they wrote with skill and dignity, and sometimes with indignation, about what they saw and felt.

The majority of black Americans, however, were not prepared to accept the challenge of a militant Claude MacKay or the exhortations of Marcus Garvey to be repatriated to Africa. They were busy becoming involved in the expanding economy of the nation, in the dizzy life before the great crash of 1929.

Apart from a few black intellectuals, the majority of the black population in the years between the two world wars found that they had to make a new accommodation to the American system, just as their forefathers had made accommodations to slavery. Their reaction was not surprising; they tried to imitate the white people they knew—or the stereotype with which they were acquainted. That meant that they accepted the white man's view of the black man and, therefore, the disparaging concept of color classification.

If the black American wanted to be integrated into the American way of life, he had to approximate the white American ideals in all respects. This led inevitably to the vain attempts to straighten the hair, bleach the skin, affect the language, and drive flashy limousines, associated with the whites. Of course, to a greater or lesser extent, these traits were found in all the black populations in the Americas, and they were by no means peculiar to the United States. The young French Martiniquian, Frantz Fanon, relates how his family always upbraided him when he lapsed from perfect French airs by telling him that he was "behaving like a Negro," who was supposed to be most undesirable in Martinique.

Whatever the black people did, they still were not acceptable to the whites. In Chicago it was said that many clubs employed men called "spotters," whose only function was to throw out those who had entered as white, who could not be so distinguished by their outward appearance. It would have been funny, had it not been so pathetic, that the so-called spotters were often those whose attempts "to pass as white" had been discovered and frustrated. In any case, the "spotters" lost their jobs when the Depression prevented many would-be patrons from attending any social club and when those who tried to attend were quite obviously not white.

In the final analysis, then, the two societies, black and white, drifted further apart during the years between the wars. The efforts of the blacks to change themselves into copies of the privileged whites only had the effect of further demeaning them in the eyes of the whites and of increasing their own frustration. The situation was getting critical when World War II radically changed the position of America in world affairs and brought the American race problem once more to the forefront of the American consciousness.

Some historians tend to overemphasize the role of the black fighting man in the wars as the primary impetus for the change in postwar race relations. This is far too simple and parochial a view. American consciousness, black and white, was part of the larger world picture in which color and race were assuming prominent proportions. Hitler's atrocities against the Jews had made people very wary of the myth of racial supremacy. A great number of intellectuals had begun to attack the way Europeans dealt with their nonwhite colonies, particularly those like India and Egypt, which had been promised independence during the 1920's. The old order was disintegrating, and the nonwhite, non-European world was rising rapidly to take its rightful place in the United Nations.

Even before the war, however, the rapid changes in the United States had made the black population something of a dilemma for the whites. Between 1910 and 1940, some 1,750,000 southern blacks had moved north and decided to stay. The greater majority were in the big cities. More than 90 percent of all the black people in the northern and western states, except Missouri, lived in big cities, with more than 47 percent of them living in New York, Chicago, Philadelphia, Detroit, Cleveland, and Pittsburgh. Although most Afro-Americans still lived in the South in 1940, the migration to the North had become very pronounced. With the massive migration came an emphasis on the social problems and limited facilities that this part of the population experienced. Segregation was, of course, the worse handicap. But the wide gap in the public health of the white and black population could no longer be hidden when the black people were concentrated in northern urban ghettos and were fast becoming health hazards for the whites as well.

World War II brought about the acceleration of the process of decolonization and a new respect and prominence for the African nations emerging from colonialism. It also brought about the Cold War between the United States and the Soviet Union. But the "uncommitted Third World" had an important part to play, and so the United States began to examine its own internal affairs with the aim of reconciling the theory and practice of democracy at home while imposing it on the outside world.

There is some connection, albeit ill-defined, between the rise of the African countries after the Second World War, the growth of independent black nations in the Caribbean during the same years, and the meteoric rise in the consciousness of the black population in the United States. Radio and television brought these events into the homes of the majority of Americans, and the presence of the United Nations in New York City further accentuated the activities of the African and West Indian nations. With a very large West Indian population resident in the United States, and with West Indians playing an important role in American and African affairs, a natural coming together of the peoples of African descent took place for a brief time in the sixties. Black Americans began to wear "Afro" hairstyles and dashiki shirts and to demand wider manifestation of African cultures and languages among their own groups, and even in the school curricula. Africa was very "in" in the 1960's.

The increasing tempo of black awareness was commensurate with the increasingly rapid pace of life in the United States during the years following World War II. The black revolution was only one facet of the wider revolutionary changes in society. The passage of the Civil Rights Act of 1964 was the climax to these changes. Given the domestic and international situation of the United States during the postwar years, it could hardly keep back the pace of legal equality for its people. To do that would be to shatter the image abroad of a land of democracy and opportunity and put the country in the uncomfortable position that South Africa now holds. With the awakened aspirations of the black people, the choice confronting the country was either greater equality or increased repression. Neither course was easy, but greater repression would have been by far the more difficult of the two. Among other things, it would have driven the vast majority of Afro-Americans into the camp of the radical and well-organized Black Muslim organization, which developed in the decade of the 1950's and sought a separate territory within the United States for themselves. Some sort of integration, therefore, promised to be the easiest solution to the racial dilemma that had been built up over nearly 450 years.

Having agitated so furiously for so long, the people were surprised that the Civil Rights Act did not prove a panacea for the nation's accumulated neglect. This was the basis for the great disillusion that set in after 1964 and led to a continuation of "long hot summers," until 1970. Northern whites had overestimated their own integration while gravely underestimating the resistance of the Southerners to integration (even though a Gallup poll taken in 1961 showed that some 76 percent of white Southerners thought that the complete integration of public facilities in the South was imminent). At the same time, the black civil rights groups moved away from the integration pattern, which they had earlier espoused, and made it uncomfortable and difficult for liberal whites to participate in the movement. Because blacks lacked the skills for new jobs, the political and economic leverage, and the wherewithal to lift themselves up from the position in which they found themselves, the two groups started to move apart again.

In reality, black and white had never been close together in the United States. Historically, the country has been divided into ethnic neighborhoods, with a well-defined hierarchical social structure in each. The black neighborhood was conspicuous in the South, where the community had the ethnic services of a black lawyer, a black priest, a black doctor, a black grocer, and a variety of black skilled and semiskilled craftsmen. In the North, however, the black neighborhoods lacked the hierarchical structure. In other words, the middle- and upper-echelon services—from skilled craftsmen to doctors, lawyers, and ministers—were provided to a greater or lesser degree by outsiders, by the whites. At the same time, the majority of the labor force of the black neighborhood worked outside their community, in factories or industries and corporations owned and controlled from the outside.

Composing a little more than 10 percent of the population, Afro-Americans controlled and held down about 2 percent of the top jobs, only 4 percent of the intermediate jobs, and more than 16 percent of the lower-echelon jobs. Low skills and lack of seniority meant that the blacks were last hired, first fired and laid off, and weakest in resisting the frequent economic downturns that the country experienced.

The system of working in one place and living in another —of integration by day and segregation by night—obviously weakens the harmonious interrelations of the groups and reduces the chances for their mutual understanding of each other. In the absence of more exposure and better understanding, the two races in the United States will continue to consider each other not in terms of what they really are but in the terms of the stereotypes and myths that undermine mutual confidence. While the situation is changing, tension will not likely disappear until the vast majority of Afro-Americans feel that they have equal opportunities for education, housing, and unrestricted entry into the professions and the trade unions from which they are still virtually barred. With better education and better skills, the Afro-American sector of the society will improve in relation to its population. This means that Afro-Americans should comprise roughly 10 percent of the scientists, 10 percent of the artists, 10 percent of the firemen, 10 percent of the lawyers, and 10 percent of the teachers. It also means that the present lily-white suburbs will have to accept roughly 10 percent of the others. This readjustment will be the most difficult one for the future Americans, but without it there can be no end to overt discrimination and segregation based on race and color. The immediate future prospects of American race relations will depend on the degree to which the majority of white Americans will accept the trained, skilled, and qualified Afro-American in their midst. In this sense, therefore, the race problem is a white problem.

The "Racial Democracy" of Brazil

Brazilians, until very recently, liked to talk about the racial democracy that their country had achieved. By this they meant no more than that the country had not found it necessary to establish the elaborate and rigid structure of laws segregating and dividing the population. They could also point to the fact that Brazilian blacks occupied some, though admittedly few, high places in the army, in government, in business, and in the professions. One of the leading modern Brazilian artists and dramatists, Abdias do Nascimento, was nonwhite. The king of Brazilian soccer—*the* Brazilian sport, and one with a far wider international appeal than either American football or baseball—Pelé, is of unmistakable African descent. Mulattoes, and other persons of mixed blood, have enjoyed a relatively great degree of social, economic, and political mobility in Brazil during the twentieth century. Superficially, then, the case seems well made.

On closer examination, Brazil presents a difference in degree, and maybe in kind, from the United States, but the talk of "racial democracy" is more a myth than a reality. At least this is the conclusion of a very large number of articulate Brazilian and foreign writers and scholars who have been doing research on the attitudes of Brazilian whites to the Afro-Brazilian population in general.

Brazil has always come up in discussions about slavery and slave societies and race relations as though it offered a natural contrast to the United States. Certainly, in some respects, a contrast exists. In general, however, the Brazilian situation offers more contradiction and greater complexity than the United States. What are the similarities, and wherein lie the differences?

As we have seen before, the historical course of slavery differed in Brazil from that of the United States. After the abolition of Brazilian slavery in 1888, race relations took a different turn. There was no open civil war as in the United States or Cuba. In contrast to the United States, Brazil had also a more homogeneous, if smaller, intellectual elite, which helped to fashion the ideals of the state. Obviously, with a majority of the population being of distinct African descent before the massive immigration of the post-1880 period, these intellectuals (and the entire Brazilian community) had to confront the problem of race. But when they came to think about race, they thought about it in ways that were different from the ways that the United States intellectuals thought about it.

To begin, there was the unmistakable demographic fact that the country was strongly African. In 1872, while slavery was still present, though waning, only about 38 percent of the population was considered by Brazilians to be "white." Only 20 percent of the population was considered to be "black," and most of these were slaves. The largest single block of Brazilians was deemed to be "mulatto"—42 percent. Since less than one-third of the population was enslaved, and since slavery was fast disappearing in the Americas, more concern was expressed about the anachronistic institution of slavery than about race before 1889.

This concern for slavery took a different course in Brazil than in the United States. In the United States the problem of slavery became quite easily a sectional dispute owing to the preponderance of the slaves in the South. All parts of Brazil participated at some time in the system of slavery. Not all regions had participated to the same extent, not all had been affected to the same degree by the importation of Africans. Everywhere in Brazil there were slaves and slaveowners, and ex-slaves and ex-slaveowners. Both the attackers and the defenders of the system of slavery in Brazil, therefore, represented the entire spectrum of the country. The problem of slavery was a national problem, not a regional one. The abolition of slavery came about after the sugar economy of the Northeast collapsed. The impoverished slaveowners found it easier to free their slaves than support them and maintain the image of the old days. They refused to ally with the new coffee elites of Rio de Janeiro and São Paulo, and instead they joined with the industrialists who wanted free men whom they could train to work on their machines. These free men, most of whom were immigrants from Germany, Italy, Portugal, and Spain, were reluctant to work alongside slaves, in any case. The new industrialists and the immigrants formed a new social group with attitudes different from the old Northeast, where both masters and slaves continued in poverty.

In a similar way, Brazilians at the turn of the century could not talk about the freedmen being a new problem in the history of their country. Brazil had always had a significant free nonwhite population consisting mainly of Africans and people of African descent. More important, however, these free colored people had already established themselves as a vital part of the Brazilian nation, attaining the very highest status in social and economic terms in the society. One mulatto, the Baron de Cotegipe, had become a nobleman and a prime minister. Another mulatto, Andre Rebouças, had been the most outstanding engineer in Brazil. Other mulattoes had achieved eminence in the country and bridged the lines of caste and class. While it is true that the blacks were by and large excluded from such mobility, there was hope that succeeding generations could do something about it by mating with persons of the higher and more acceptable classes. The mulatto, then, offered a safety valve for ambitions and escape. That the mulattoes and free blacks "whitened" themselves is reflected in the census returns that showed a stable black percentage between 1890 and 1940, somewhere in the region of 15 percent of the entire Brazilian population. But in some regions, especially cities such as Rio de Janeiro, the percentage of blacks in the population declined steadily. Obviously, the blacks either passed as white or were dying out. The latter possibility seems more plausible, as the older slaves died without offspring.

The Brazilians found themselves in a dilemma after the abolition of slavery. They were predominantly an Africanized nation, yet they were influenced by and they accepted white European ideals. This dilemma is characterized by the ambivalence of Brazilian thinking in the latter part of the nineteenth century and the early decades of the twentieth. During this period, Brazilian intellectual thought moved in three main directions.

In the first place, some Brazilians accepted the fact that the slaves and the free African and Indian elements of the population were different but not necessarily inferior to the white. Actually, this pattern of thought was most dominant before the abolition of slavery, and it lent some support to the abolitionist and humanitarian cause. Unlike the defenders of slavery in the United States who, more often than not, stated the view that Africans were biologically inferior and therefore predestined to perpetual slavery, the Brazilians generally saw slavery—as did the Cubans at the same time—as merely the best solution (and to some, the only solution) to the acute shortage of labor. In other words, no slavery meant no economic development.

The second argument saw slavery as a handicap to the country since it inhibited the free flow of European immigrants to Brazil by depressing wages. This was undesirable, and so not surprisingly the staunchest abolitionists, men such as José de Patrocinio and Joaquim Nabuco argued that Brazil would never realize its true potential until the slaves gained their freedom and European immigrants were brought into the country. It is noteworthy that very few abolitionists saw the slaves as playing a role in the future of Brazil; and only one, Andre Rebouças, put forward a plan whereby the ex-slaves would be used as trained wage earners in agriculture and industry.

Then there was a third argument, an argument that was more thoroughly racist than the other two and one that was very common in the Americas during the latter half of the nineteenth century. Rather than speak directly of race, the Brazilians, and some leading Hispanic Americans, used the euphemism "civilization." The argument took a curious turn. Instead of speaking of Africans, Indians, and persons of mixed blood, the intellectuals spoke about the conflict between civilization and barbarism. The glittering cities and the Europeans represented civilization. All the rest was barbarism. In the 1870's and 1880's, Nabuco and Patricinio condemned the plans to import East Indians as laborers, declaring that they were no better than the Africans and would only aggravate the social problem. What Brazil needed, they insisted, was a constant stream of European immigrants, especially from the northern part of Europe. The unspoken assumption then, but one that reached full flower with the lyrical prose of Gilberto Freyre during the 1930's, was that the European immigrants would gradually whiten the Brazilian population, and the social problem of the African and Indian element would naturally pass away.

The espousal of the idea of a gradual whitening of the population by European immigration was an acknowledgment that this was more desirable than building a Brazil based on the predominantly mixed groups that occupied it at the time. This view reflected the position of Brazilian positivists and other European racists that the Africans and Indians were inferior to the Europeans. The Brazilians, therefore, in advertising the attractions of their country abroad during the early years of the Republic, played down the multiracial nature of their country and emphasized the European resemblances of the south: the terrain, the climate, and the freedom from occupational competition. When Brazilians joined the Europeans in espousing racism toward the end of the nineteenth century—as almost all Latin American intellectuals did—they did it with a difference. Racial determinism would condemn them and their country, and so some found an escape route.

Brazil had a long history of multiracial contact. It had too obvious an experience of achievement and high status cutting across all racial lines to accept entirely a foreign concept of racial inferiority. The whitening theory was, in a sense, a compromise. While the ideal was to have a white Brazil, the attempts would be made to whiten the nonwhite, not to eliminate them or ignore them.

Eventually, the Brazilians turned away from racism around the time of the World War I and decided to build their nationalism on diversity and peculiarity. It was not a sudden decision, and it was not clear until the 1930's that the argument had really changed, that something approaching "Brazil is beautiful" had replaced the indiscriminate acceptance that white was right, good, and best. This change in the Brazilian position came about as the result of many circumstances. Brazil was being surpassed by Argentina in the search for European immigrants. Brazilian participation in World War I politicized many black and white Americans from all parts of the New World. About the time of the war, too, as we mentioned already, the Europeans and the North Americans were beginning to have second thoughts about the validity of scientific racism. That people were different could not be disputed. But who could determine who was inferior and who was superior? This doubt left an opening for a number of Brazilian writers to rush in and declare that there was some virtue in the multiracial society. Brazilians began to decide that they would shape a nationalism according to their own experience and local conditions. The divergence with the North American experience became more pronounced.

The turning away from overt racism did not mean the end of prejudice and discrimination but merely the rejection of rigid and manifest segregation. The ideals and highest values of the Brazilian society still remained white biased. Nevertheless, after 1920, there could be no direct racial confrontation. For if the Brazilians were to use multiracialism as an integral part of their incipient nationalism, then they could not engage in racist politics at the same time—at least the state could not be overtly racist. Discrimination continued, but in a subtle form, and no one ever thought segregation by race possible or necessary.

The absence of direct racial confrontation has led Brazilian and non-Brazilian writers to conclude that Brazil enjoys a "racial democracy." The absence of racial tension does not mean that prejudice does not exist or that the black Brazilians are fully accepted into the society. Indeed, the history of Brazil in the twentieth century has been one of a society in which color and class have played significant roles, and continue to play significant roles. The society is white biased, and many subtle forms of discrimination exist against the black and the mulatto populations. During the 1920's and after, a number of predominantly black civil rights organizations sprang up claiming to defend the rights of the underprivileged sector of the society—basically the Afro-Brazilians. The constant, if short lived, proliferation of these groups and organizations belies the tranquil and harmonious relations of the races in Brazil. Florestan Fernandez and Carl Degler have described a number of the forms of discrimination that exist in Brazil. Many other studies clearly reflect the racial bias of the majority of the population from school-age children up to and including adults and civil servants. Any traveler in Brazil today will admit that the black population comprises the lowest paid, the hardest worked, and the most marginal of the social groups. This does not necessarily reflect discrimination. But a group uniformly classified at the bottom of the society must reflect a stereotype that fosters discrimination and neglect.

It is interesting to speculate on the reasons for the failure of the protest organizations in Brazil, which would form rough equivalents to the black protest and civil rights organizations in the United States. Some of these organizations in the United States go back almost seventy years. None in Brazil has survived a decade without disintegration and reform. Why did these organizations fail to form a continuing part of Brazilian social life?

The answer to this question lies in the varied interrelated factors of Brazilian life, politics, and history. In the first place, Brazil does not have the same degree of party cohesion and consistency that has been a part of United States political life since the nineteenth century. The failure of long-lasting political parties says something about the conditions characterizing political life in Brazil and suggests that any organization that has political ambitions, or depends on politics for survival, would meet the same fate as the political parties.

Brazil has a long history of organized military or oligarchic hostility to political parties. From time to time, political parties have been banned, and naturally all organizations that embrace a large group would fall under suspicion and probably be banned. This is exactly what happened to the best and strongest black civil rights organization ever formed in Brazil, the *Frente Negra Brasileiro*, the Brazilian Negro Front. This was a group formed by about 2,000 persons in São Paulo in 1931. The Brazilian Negro Front declared that it was a "political and social union of the black national people . . . to declare their social and political rights in the Brazilian community in the present." It was growing in membership when it was suddenly declared by the government of Getulio Vargas to be illegal, along with all other political parties. The group dissolved and resurfaced as the National Union of the Men of Color of São Paulo. Presumably, it did not declare itself to be a political party like its predecessor. Obviously, the black civil rights organizations were vulnerable to the local political conditions.

In the second place, civil rights organizations were designed to fight discrimination rather than overt legal disabilities and segregation, and they were weak because they had great difficulty identifying the forms of abuses that they wanted to eliminate. The subtle forms of Brazilian prejudice do not lend themselves to the militant organization of a party or a group. The mulatto has always had open opportunities. All men of means are free to engage in any social organization, and no laws explicitly forbid the activities of any group. Moreover, a strong, popular myth prevails that prejudice does not exist. It is difficult to get people excited about race. Even the people who are discriminated against fail to display much enthusiasm for civil rights organizations that articulate their disabilities. In 1951 the government of Brazil passed a civil rights law, the Afonso Arinos Law. This was designed to remove the discrimination that the Congress agreed existed despite the 1946 constitution. Brazilian opinion is still divided over the effectiveness of this law.

The racial paradox of Brazil, therefore, is that the situation is both more difficult and easier than that in the United States of America. Because it is subtle, it is more difficult to erase. Nevertheless, this subtlety makes it less unpleasant for both the practitioner and the recipient of discrimination. The situation cannot be substantially remedied until the general condition of the black population is economically improved. For the preponderance of the black people at the bottom of the economic and social ladder perpetuates the forms of discrimination. The elimination of discrimination requires a radical restructuring of the Brazilian society. There has been no radical restructuring of the Brazilian society during the twentieth century, and there are no likely prospects that this is about to happen.

Hope exists that greater industrialization might offer the economic opportunities for the black and underprivileged to break out of their mold. Statistical evidence for Bahia, a predominantly black and backward state, and for São Paulo, an industrialized and progressive state, suggests that with greater participation in the economy, the black population quickly seeks to redress its educational and social disabilities. Bahia is about 70 percent black. Only about 7 percent of the São Paulo population is black. While the national percentage of black high school graduates is just 11 percent, São Paulo alone supplies nearly 7 percent of the national figure. Clearly, the opportunities in São Paulo exceed by far those elsewhere.

It would seem reasonable to argue, along with Brazilians such as Florestan Fernandez, that industrialization is the most important factor for the thorough integration of the state. However, there is no guarantee that this will be the end result. The more industrialized cities and states of Brazil have been the ones with the fewest black and mulatto people and the greatest degree of racial discrimination and prejudice. The greater the economic competition, therefore, the greater may be the growth of prejudice and discrimination. The settler mentality of southern Brazil could follow the pattern of the United States. It could be that Brazilian whites may regard the educated black worker as a threat and, therefore, move in the direction of excluding him, especially in the unions and workers' cooperatives. Given the history of Brazil, however, this is unlikely to reach the extreme form prevalent in the United States of America.

Cuba

Cuba and Puerto Rico offer different variations of the present situations of the Afro-Americans in the contemporary societies of the Western Hemisphere. The two islands were, until 1898, colonies of Spain, but their importance and their history took slightly different turns during the nineteenth century. In both, the sugar revolution of the period had tremendous impact, but the socioracial consequences were quite dissimilar. Cuba followed the path of Brazil and the other West Indian islands where sugar at some time was "king." Puerto Rico followed the path of the smaller, more commercial islands such as the Bahamas, the Lesser Antilles, and Dutch Curaçao and Aruba.

As we saw earlier, when we looked at the history of slavery in Cuba, the consequence of the large-scale production of sugar was the virtual innundation of the white population by Africans. By the middle of the nineteenth century, the Afro-Cuban population had surpassed the white population. The fear that Cuba was being "Africanized" extended beyond the awareness that there were more people of African descent in the island than any others. The culture of Cuba was also affected. The music, cuisine, and religion became enriched by the vital elements of African culture transmitted by the large numbers of Africans who were brought to the island as slaves to work on the plantations and in the cities. Associations of Africans kept alive a Cuban version of the life and style of Africa, and each town in the island had its African *barrio,* or section. At times the government tried to suppress these essentially African activities, but always in vain. In taverns, secret societies, welfare organizations, and in the homes, the Africans kept alive their image of Africa. This image, however, slowly became more and more an idealized version as the Africans became more and more Cuban.

The retention of Africanisms was not the only factor affecting the Afro-Cuban population that survived slavery, and it was probably not the most important factor at all. The social system of slavery and the Spanish colony affected the Afro-Cuban population in much the same way that the conditions of Portuguese life and society affected the Brazilian people of all colors. In Cuba, just as in Brazil, the people of African descent formed one sector of a hierarchically arranged social structure. Race and color were distinguishing characteristics, but each sector had its rights and privileges. What is more, an overlap occurred, just as in the Brazilian case, making Cuba and Brazil a combination of settler and nonsettler societies. This racial and color overlap allowed for a certain degree of mobility between the different strata of society, strata that the Spanish called *castes*.

By the end of slavery in 1886, the free people of color formed nearly 16 percent of the total population of Cuba. The greatest concentration of these people were outside the zones of the plantations, for they, like the poor whites, had insufficient capital to engage in sugar, coffee, and commerce on a large scale. But they managed to play a significant role in the life of the colony, dominating the skills and urban services that were either undersupplied or neglected by the white population. In common with other American societies, the free colored population was largely urban based. Nevertheless, in the eastern part of the island, which had not yet been overrun by the sugar plantations toward the end of the century, the free colored population accounted for a substantial part of the labor force and ranked among the property owners. The highest density of free colored people was found in the eastern part of the island.

As in Brazil, the free colored population had achieved a remarkable degree of economic and social acceptance in the country, even though the great majority of the people retained a bias towards the ideals of the white Europeans and Americans. Black people, or at any rate, mulattoes, had become medical doctors—even though that had been forbidden under the colonial laws—and had excelled in painting and literature. Before Antonio Maceo, Máximo Gómez, and the other brilliant military leaders of the Ten Years' War (1868-1878) had won plaudits for their race and their cause, all Cubans and many Spaniards had heard of the poetry of Gabriel de la Concepción Valdés, better known as "Plácido." Plácido (d. 1844) certainly ranks high among Cuban poets, and he was perhaps the first really well-known poet from the island. Toward the latter part of the nineteenth century, therefore, the situation of the free colored in Brazil and Cuba was proceeding along parallel paths. In Cuba, however, the seeds of sharp division had already been planted.

In Cuba, the pressures to abolish slavery came from the outside. The great Cuban planters had, however, won concessions from the metropolis that their economy would not be undermined by any rash action such as the sudden abolition of slavery. As early as 1847, therefore, the Cubans were given permission to import Mexican Indians and Chinese to work on the plantations and supply the labor for which the slaves were insufficient and the free colored population reluctant. These Mexican Indians and the Chinese were classified as "white" at the time. Plantation labor was commonly believed to be "black man's work," and it had the lowest prestige among all forms of labor. With the Mexicans and Chinese doing some part of the demanding physical toil of the plantations, the sharp identification of a particular type of work with race could not be maintained. Instead, what happened was that the Mexicans and the Chinese inherited the demeaned status formerly assigned to the slaves, and along with that, all the derogatory descriptions and insinuations. The Chinese and the Mexicans were a minority in the population-at-large, and the unfortunate stereotypes flourished. It became increasingly accepted that some members of the free colored community were higher in social status, economic condition, and general acceptance than a certain group of "white" persons, even if this were not true for all in the free colored community. This had the effect of diluting the inflexibility toward race and color that might otherwise have developed in the society-at-large. It also meant that the society was moving away from the polarization along lines of race and color that had been the experience in the United States of America. Cuban nationalism, therefore, like Brazilian nationalism at the turn of the twentieth century, could hardly adopt a "pure white" policy. The Cubans began to think as early as the late 1860's that the solution of the race problem would likely be in the increasing whitening of the black population. The Cubans assumed, as did the Brazilians, that the superiority of the white genes would settle the matter.

The implication of white superiority inherent in any assumption of such a process of resolving race relations carries with it some acceptance of integration, at least integration of blood types, and a certain promiscuity in sexual relations. The Cuban-born white tended to think, like his Brazilian counterpart, that the mulatto had a certain sexual attraction and beauty that was irresistible. This is clearly brought out in a novel of the period, *Cecilia Valdés,* written by Cirilo Villaverde, and first published in 1882. Villaverde manages to trace the nuances of race and color in the fading period of the colonial society, near the end of slavery. Black was out; the mulatto was definitely acceptable as a bedmate, though not a marriage partner.

The attitudes toward race and color in the Cuban society at the end of the nineteenth century were fundamentally those of the Spanish and Iberian society, modified continually throughout the colonial period. As such, they were akin to those of the Portuguese. At the end of the century, the North Americans moved into Cuba, bringing political power and social conduct to bear on a region where only their capital had penetrated before. With the intensive North American penetration came an entirely different concept of race and color. Sugar manufacturing became an even bigger business than it had been before, eliminating marginal producers, establishing large sugar factories, called *Centrales,* and expelling people from the land in an inexorable movement eastward from Havana to Santiago de Cuba. After the occupation of Cuba by the United States armed forces, the Americans began a new color classification of the people, which relegated the Mexicans and Chinese to the category of "colored" and sharpened the discrimination between the colors on the island. By their clubs and their behavior, the Americans infused a good deal of the traditions of the North American mainland in the island of Cuba. White Cubans, too, began to be more fastidious about color in order to be more acceptable to the North Americans.

The color consciousness that accompanied the North Americans to Cuba was only one facet of a process whereby the free colored population found themselves in a rapidly deteriorating situation. As long as it was possible to find open land to cultivate in the eastern part of the island, a number of people, black as well as white, could operate outside the cash economy. Working periodically on the estates, and supplementing this income by the produce of minor plots cultivated around their homes, or under sufferance of the big planters, these people managed to eke out a miserable existence. With the process of sugar manufacture more mechanized, there was little room for small farming on the estates. Marginal agriculturalists worked as cutters of the sugar cane during the few months of harvest. Many of them had little or no schooling, and the estates were not interested in providing schools or health services. The condition of these people slowly became worse as the success of sugar became greater.

By the middle of the twentieth century the condition of the black person in Cuba was pathetic. The island became almost singularly preoccupied with the production of sugar. Most food and equipment were imported. United States machine-made products drove out the small, skilled artisans, such as shoemakers and cabinetmakers. Even cigarettes were made by machines. The black people formed a core of unemployed and unemployable in the society. From time to time the government mouthed felicitous phrases promising a new deal for all the poor, especially the people of color. This was usually just before, or just after, a change in government. Nothing concrete was done for the poor and the black in Cuba, even though the successive governments tried hard not to have a repetition of the vicious race riots that occurred in 1909, when some 3,000 persons—all black—lost their lives.

The black population predominated among the poor, and all the poor were callously neglected by the government and the "big people" in Havana. There was no overt racial segregation, but there was the same type of debilitating discrimination that existed for Brazil. The hotels, clubs, restaurants, gambling houses, and commercial establishments of the

Informal cooperative labor on field day. *(Research Institute for the Study of Man, New York)*

cities—especially those which catered to the Americans —refused to hire any colored person except in the basest occupations, claiming that it was bad for business. In 1949, no black person featured among the upper echelons of the labor unions, the police, the military, or the government, although Cubans themselves denied the existence of discrimination. It was, however, virtually impossible for any black person to overcome the subtle forms of discrimination that marred his every step.

The trend the Cuban socioracial situation had taken could only be reversed by a revolutionary restructuring of the society, in which all the poor and the blacks could be given opportunities for upliftment and ennoblement. This is what Fidel Castro tried to do. Obviously, the Castro Revolution moved considerably toward undermining discrimination and prejudice by imposing equality of status among all the people. The sense of participation in the revolution, which stimulated so many Cubans, was especially pronounced among the black minority. Before 1959 they felt themselves to be the forgotten sector of the Cuban society. The revolution created new opportunities for decent labor, for equal education, and for rewarding and challenging jobs in the military, in government, in the foreign service, and in every phase of Cuban public life.

Most Cubans today admit that the status and acceptability of the Cuban population have improved markedly. The high proportion of Afro-Cubans among the upper echelon of the revolutionary administration testifies to that. Nevertheless, the continuing small number of racially mixed marriages still accentuates the tenacious vestiges of discrimination that remain in the private lives of a considerable number of Cubans. The perfectly integrated society is a matter of time and steadfast application.

During the late 1960's many of the Black Panther sympathizers from the United States who fled to Cuba, such as John Clytus, who wrote *Black Man in Red Cuba,* complained that the island society was just as racist as the United States. This claim seems to be patently false. The Panthers probably interpreted political differences as manifestations of racism. If they were unwelcome in Cuba, it was less because of their color than of their political philosophy. Cuban socialists and the Black Panthers had widely varying programs and problems. And neither side made clear the real roots of their mutual discontent.

As long as the Castro Revolution is a reality, Cuba will continue to provide a most favorable environment for the Afro-Cuban sector of the population. It seems likely that equality of justice, economic opportunities, and political participation will eventually remove all the differences between the Afro-Cubans and the Euro-Cubans and accelerate the racial integration of the society. In any case, the revolution represents the first attempt to de-emphasize the racial divisions in the society. Cuban socialism, by creating, or at least attempting to create, a new society has effectively removed the traditional social cleavages based on race, color, and economic position.

Puerto Rico

Perhaps nowhere has the negative effect of the United States of America on race relations been more pronounced than in the small Caribbean island of Puerto Rico. While never a racial paradise, it was a place where race had been minimal until the island fell under the direct political and economic sphere of the United States at the beginning of the twentieth century.

Puerto Rico had never participated to the same extent in the transatlantic slave trade as had those other islands such as Cuba, Barbados, Jamaica, and Hispaniola where sugar had been the mainstay at some stage or the other in their historical development. Even though Puerto Rico underwent the sugar revolution, at no time in the island's history did the slaves exceed 14 percent of the total island population. And even when the sugar revolution was at its height during the nineteenth century, its social and demographic effect was considerably less than that of Cuba. Puerto Rico had few really great sugar cane estates; very few with more than fifty slaves. Instead, the principal agricultural enterprises were coffee and small crops, which involved neither considerable capital outlays nor considerable labor requirements. The black and colored population increased from 12.5 percent of the total population in 1765 to 33 percent in 1794; to 53 percent in 1802; and it declined slowly after that to 50 percent in 1827; 48 percent in 1860; 34 percent in 1910; and 23 percent in 1950 (see Table 4). Increased white immigration and "passing as white" explain some of the decline in the black population. Slavery in Puerto Rico, therefore, was not an important economic enterprise; and the absence of the large slave-operated plantation had a salutary effect on the population as a whole.

TABLE 4   *Black and Mulatto Population in Puerto Rico*

Year	Percentage of island population
1765	12.5
1794	33.0
1802	53.0
1827	50.0
1860	48.0
1910	34.0
1950	23.0
1960	20.0

Throughout the nineteenth century Puerto Rico had a large proportion of mulattoes, amounting to nearly 33 percent of the population. And even though the number of slaves more than doubled during the early decades of the nineteenth century when agricultural activity intensified, the slaves played an ever-decreasing role in the labor force. By and large, the Puerto Rican planters merely reorganized the large population of free mulattoes and free blacks, accentuated the distinctions between landed and landless, and coerced the landless to supply the labor required on the great estates. By so doing, the planters and slaveowners were seldom short of a labor force and were not afraid to abolish slavery in their island, as were the Cubans. Unlike the Brazilian Northeast, Puerto Rico was not impoverished by the collapse of sugar. The slaveowners in Puerto Rico were among the forefront of the abolitionists in the Spanish *Cortes* of the late 1860's and succeeded in winning the total emancipation with indemnity of their slaves by 1873. After that the exslaves joined the coerced free labor force on the plantations, and as Rafael Maria Labra described, "The planters continued without losing a single day's labor."

By 1898, when the United States arrived in Puerto Rico, there was not a single facet of Puerto Rican life in which the black and mulatto population had not equally distinguished themselves. In 1900 more than 33 percent of the property owners in Puerto Rico were either black or mulatto. But what is more important is that there was no distinction of labor or any other activity based on racial or color characteristics. It seemed that Puerto Rico had been furthest toward achieving that "racial democracy" that had eluded all the other postslavery New World societies.

The changes under the United States administration were subtle and gradual. The multiracial oligarchy, which had welcomed the Americans with open arms, attempted to copy them "without bothering to be selective about anything," as the Puerto Rican scholar Juan Rodriguez Cruz described it. Discriminations based on race or color, while not actively foisted by the North Americans upon the Puerto Ricans (as it had been in Cuba), were part and parcel of the cultural baggage that the Puerto Ricans willingly accepted. Schools, clubs, hotels, banks, businesses, and private gatherings began to be slowly segregated according to color. The situation had become so bad in 1946 that the Puerto Rican legislature had to pass a special bill forbidding racial discrimination in public places against any person on account of race or color or creed, although this had previously been outlawed by the 1942 Civil Rights Law. In 1945 three persons were brought to justice for discrimination against three blacks in a San Juan nightclub. As late as 1950, when the discussions surrounding the Constitution of the Associated Free Statehood of Puerto Rico were being held (and the last year in which the Puerto Ricans established racial divisions in their decennial census), Juan Falu Zarzuela was badgering the committee in behalf of his *Liga para el Progreso de la Gente de Color en Puerto Rico*

Vendor in marketplace. *(Research Institute for the Study of Man, New York)*

(Association for the Advancement of the Colored People of Puerto Rico) to write in guarantees of the civil rights of the Puerto Rican nonwhites. His argument was that, although the situation had been steadily improving since 1942, the nonwhite Puerto Ricans had a long way to go and were still encountering discrimination of various sorts throughout the island. Black organizations in Puerto Rico succeeded no better than in Brazil. Not political hostility but public apathy undermined them.

Many prominent Puerto Ricans have from time to time denied the existence of racial discrimination in the island. As early as 1909, Dr. José Celso Barbosa, a medical doctor trained at the University of Michigan in Ann Arbor, declared that Puerto Rico had no color prejudice. As a prominent physician and a wealthy man, he had, of course, encountered no such prejudice and discrimination. But the situation was not the same for the greater majority of the Puerto Rican nonwhites. A study carried out by the University of Puerto Rico in 1958 found that racial prejudice was a pervasive part of Puerto Rican life. Well over 50 percent of the white Puerto Ricans claimed that they would not like to live beside a black family or have a member of their family marry into a black family. Blacks were employed only at the lower levels of business and industry. Two industrial firms admitted that they did not usually employ "colored persons," and not a single bank in the four largest Puerto Rican towns had any colored person among those employees who attended the public. In San Juan, the capital of Puerto Rico, only four of the eighty-five concerns investigated had any nonwhite employees.

In 1958 Puerto Rico did not offer any better prospects for the nonwhite than Cuba or parts of the United States. The price for admission to the North American Union was the establishment of a socioracial code, which made North Americans very comfortable in Puerto Rico. Since 1959 the government has been moving actively against discrimination in public facilities, and the island has been caught up in the revolution of civil rights encountered by the mainland during the 1960's.

Puerto Rico is currently undergoing a wave of nationalism. In the universities, as well as in the community-at-large, more and more people are being attracted to the idea that the country should go it alone, should break the bonds with the United States, and establish itself as a distinct nation within the family of the United Nations. There is, however, a strong counterforce in the great number who prefer statehood for the island. Since independence would mean a rapid deterioration in the standard of living in Puerto Rico—which, as Oscar Lewis described in *La Vida,* is very low in the growing slums—and tremendous difficulties for any government trying to compete openly in the North American market without the advantages of the *Asociado Estado Libre* (Associated Free State) arrangements, statehood seems the more likely course in the future. But as a state of the United States of America, the tendency toward accepting the norms of the mainland would be even greater than before.

It seems unlikely that Puerto Rico will be able to resist the pressures to model the island's development and social values after the majority of the American public—an essentially white, Protestant, affluent, and materialist public. This course will in all probability result in the hardening of racial attitudes and in distinctions based on race and color. Already the Puerto Rican "white" is regarded in New York as a minority group and is treated in many cases as an inferior type of citizen. The Afro-Puerto Rican, therefore, stands no chance. His handicaps exceed those of the so-called white Puerto Rican. The future for the Afro-Puerto Rican will probably be closely tied to that of all the non-European minority groups in the United States, unless Puerto Rico breaks away and decides to throw in its lot with the other emerging nation-states of the Caribbean.

The British Caribbean

As products of nonsettler America, the British West Indies have been the most predominantly black regions of the New World. Unlike the Spanish islands of Cuba and Puerto Rico, or Brazil, the English Antilles were left at the end of slavery with a small and declining white population.

The historical legacy of slavery differed in the British West Indies from the Anglo-Saxon North American mainland. Because the islands and Guyana were not settlement colonies, the number of white women venturing out to the region was very small. The white men had never really looked on the territories as home, and so they often left their wives in England, or in North America. If they did by chance bring their families, or if they created families after their arrival, they were always anxious to send their children back to the mother country where they could be "properly educated" and satisfactorily mated. Otherwise, the white population constituted a predominantly male population seeking the fortune, like the Pinney family of eighteenth-century Nevis, that would allow them to return to their native land and actively participate in their own society. The absence of women made for a certain laxity in relations with such women as were found in the islands. After a time, it was expected, and fashionable, for Englishmen to accept Afro-West Indian housekeepers, whose status was actually that of a common-law wife. This liaison of white and black spawned the large number of free colored, the profile of which we looked at when we examined slavery in the British West Indies in Chapter 2.

The British West Indian model that developed after slavery was closer to the Ibero-American than to the North American society. Yet there was a significant difference. Throughout the West Indies, black men and mulattoes had assumed positions of importance. The teaching, medical, legal, bureaucratic, police, and military establishments were dominated by the blacks. By the beginning of the twentieth century, therefore, the groundwork had been laid for the assumption of political power that came with the withdrawal from the British empire. The British West Indian blacks formed the majority population, reflecting a majority consciousness. Along with Haiti, this was a unique American development. But the societies were dominated economically by white people, and the entire region—except for Trinidad with its petroleum resources—was a vulnerable competitor on the international market.

Perhaps it was the "majority consciousness" of the British West Indians that fed the myths that race and color had no place in the West Indies. West Indians themselves claimed that their islands presented the model of harmonious interracial cooperation, the living examples of the success of the plural society. Part of the reason for these claims was the desire to make the island attractive to foreign tourists, although a great many people genuinely believed the islands had no color and race problems.

Compared to England, to the United States, or to South Africa, the situation in the islands was undoubtedly extremely relaxed. No legal sanctions prevailed against any particular group; and after the rise of nationalism in the late 1950's, no social sanctions have been present to exclude any particular group from any place. Private preferences and discriminations, of course, exist in a way that is difficult to document or study. West Indians, too, were not conscious of the explosiveness of race until the civil war occurred in British Guiana (as Guyana was then called) in the early 1960's. Guyana remains among the few places in the Caribbean where race still engenders significant social and political sentiments.

The myths of the West Indian multiracial harmony have been and are being attacked from all quarters in the islands. Nevertheless, the consensus among academics is that race is not the chief agent of discrimination and prejudice. Color has far more meaning among the islanders than race. This is not strange, since so few people can claim to be of any one race, especially the much-preferred white race. The islands have a mixed population, and that much is obvious to the eye as one travels from place to place. In the larger islands, especially Jamaica, Barbados, and Trinidad, the black populations are large and distinct from the mulattoes, but in others such as Dominica, St. Lucia, St. Vincent, and Grenada, the variations of light-skinned people present a marvelous variety. Shades of color, not race per se, therefore, are the chief preoccupations of the islands.

The color prejudice that exists in the islands is a very complex one. It is not just the mere color of skin that is used to classify people. Other external attributes feature prominently in West Indian classifications, such as the straightness of the nose, the physical build of the individual, or the "quality" of a person's hair. In general, West Indians envisage a scale running from the highly preferred "European" features to the usually despised "African" features. But even so, the different

Fishermen in Jamaica. (*Research Institute for the Study of Man, New York*)

factors are weighted differently from place to place, and so
the degree of skin color might be easily offset by the absence
of some of the other desirable traits. Local population compos-
tion also plays a part in race and color consciousness.

In Trinidad, for example, the East Indians are a closely knit
group, differing in race and religion, and in community relations, from the rest of the population. Nevertheless, the small
geographical size of the island and the greater racial mixture
in occupation and opportunities create less friction and
mutual suspicion than in Guyana where the Afro-West Indians and the East Indians have far fewer points of contact
within the society.

The dominant political party of Trinidad, the People's National Movement, headed by the eminent historian, Eric Williams, is a far more multiracial party of all the Trinidadian
people than is the People's National Congress of Prime Minister Forbes Burnham in Guyana, which, apart from being
more thoroughly black, represents a minority racial party.
Both in Trinidad and in Guyana, however, the government
places great stress on national cohesion as a desirable goal.
Guyana's goal of "One People, One Nation" seems, however,
to be farther from realization than Trinidad's "Together we
aspire. Together we achieve." Apart from Trinidad and
Guyana, political parties with openly racial appeal have not
made much headway in the other islands. In Jamaica, which
spurned Marcus Garvey in the 1930's, neither Millard Johnson, a follower of Garvey, nor the Ras Tafari, a millennial
sect, proved able to channel appeals of racial solidarity via a
functioning or successful political party. Even in Barbados,
which has a more solid color grouping, the political parties
and the trade unions have made appeals across these lines.

On the other hand, in the small islands, especially Grenada
and the Grenadines, Antigua, Nevis, Anguilla, St. Kitts, and
Montserrat, color and race are less important than genealogy.
The islands themselves are so small and the families so well
known and established that physical appearance matters far
less than family descent. Indeed, it is hardly an exaggeration
to say that in these islands everybody knows everybody else.
The lines of social class and caste are therefore relatively
fixed and handed down from generation to generation.

Despite the fact that the societies of the larger islands have been "open" for the last 140 or so years, the majority of the people are poor. The elites, regardless of color, have never bothered to attempt any restructuring of the societies in order to alleviate the poverty and decreasing ability to survive of the majority. These poor people tend to see their state as the result of racial and color prejudice or exploitation by the white. In the British West Indies, as in Brazil, "whiteness" can be translated into "rich." In other words, there is throughout the Caribbean a close correlation between class and color, a correlation that has not significantly changed with the coming of political independence. Everywhere, the rich have been getting richer, and the poor have been getting poorer. Everywhere, too, the majority of the poor are black, even though in some places, such as the small French island of St. Bartholemy, the entire population is practically all white. On the other hand, in other islands, such as Carriacou or Barbuda, almost all the residents of the island are black.

In general, the elites throughout the Caribbean are multiracial. Nevertheless, they tend to be predominantly fair in color and are often foreign in conduct and culture to the masses. Owing to the stratification of the local resources along these lines of color and race, the accumulated frustrations of the poor often find release in explosive riots which take on certain dimensions of color or race. Nowhere, however, do these become exclusively black versus white confrontations. Rather, the vandalism is directed against any commercial group that is recognized as the "oppressor" of the poor: Dutch and black in Curaçao; Portuguese and East Indian in Guyana and Trinidad; Chinese in Jamaica. Perhaps only in Barbados would it be conceivable that a black versus white confrontation would be possible, since most—though by no means all—of the big Barbados businessmen are white or very fair in skin color.

More and more, however, the black masses in the British Caribbean are voicing criticism of the white and colored elites that rule them and control almost every facet of the islands' culture and resources. Unfortunately, the movements from "below" tend to be captured by the very middle and upper classes that they tend to replace, and instead of having geniune change, one finds at best an expansion of the elite by a seduction of mass leadership.

The most serious concern of Caribbean society is not race, as it is understood in the United States of America. Rather, it is a variegated system of color and class. But the popular concept that the Caribbean is an area *par excellence* of the complacent plural society needs considerable qualification. The situation varies from island to island.

Race and color assume minor significance in relatively homogeneous societies such as Barbuda, Carriacou, and St. Bartholemy. On the other small islands, such as Bequia, Saba, and the Saintes, the groups of whites, coloreds, and blacks form tightly segregated groups, with the white colonists being largely expatriots. In the French islands, particularly Martinique and Guadeloupe, the local whites form a self-centered endogamous group, impervious to both French-born whites as well as the fair-skinned colored who could "pass as white." Color and lineage have paramount importance in fixing social positions, while class and occupation seem to be discounted heavily. On the other hand, in some islands the poor whites are not part of the elites but are closely affiliated with the black masses in culture, occupation, and status. This is true of the German descendants in southwestern Jamaica, of the "red leg" whites of Barbados, and the poor white groups in Grenada, St. Vincent, Guadeloupe, and St. Thomas. In Trinidad, Grenada, St. Vincent, Dominica, Barbados, Antigua, and Jamaica, the elites include large numbers of black and light-skinned persons. And almost everywhere, political power rests in the hands of black persons: The political kaleidoscope in 1971 featured Oscar Pindling in the Bahamas; Hugh Shearer in Jamaica; Paul Southwell in St. Kitts-Nevis; George Walters in Antigua; Errol Barrow in Barbados; Eric Gairy in Grenada; John Compton in St. Lucia; and Eric Williams in Trinidad and Tobago. Haiti, of course, had been controlled for a number of years by François "Papa Doc" Duvalier, who died in 1971, shortly after declaring his teen-aged son president for life.

The accession of blacks to positions of political power in the Caribbean has not affected the economic elites, who are mainly white and foreign. From the Bahamas in the north to the Guyanas in the south, the local economies are controlled by foreign interests. Everywhere except Cuba, tourism is flaunted as a necessary dollar earner to all the islands. Abroad and at home expensive campaigns are mounted to woo foreigners to the islands and to brainwash the local people into thinking that tourism matters to them. Actually, tourism is largely controlled by outside corporations that export most of the profits. A study in the United States of the tourist industry of the British Caribbean found that 77 cents of every tourist dollar was sent back abroad. At the same time, tourism inflated the cost of living tremendously and raised the price of land and commodities so much that it was outside the reach of the ordinary citizen.

Mass discontent, racial, political, and economic, finds its most articulate expression in the newly arrived black power movements throughout the region. Although strongly influenced by the North American counterpart, and while largely using the rhetoric of the United States, black power in the Caribbean is not restricted to people of African descent. Instead, it tries to speak for all the poor people wherever they may be found. The leadership tends to be middle class and college trained. Local conditions determine the format of the appeal. In Trinidad and Guyana the movement has incorporated whites as well as the poor East Indians, largely the estate workers who are grossly underpaid. In Barbados and Jamaica the movement is urban and predominantly black. Throughout the region, the movement speaks for and to the nearly 90 percent of the population who are unemployed, underemployed, ill-fed, ill-housed, and ill-clad. In Trinidad, where the black power movement had its largest appeal and greatest success in attempting to overturn the political power structure (Trinidad, incidentally, is the most prosperous Caribbean island), European Trinidadians earn an average income of $300 per month, while Afro-Trinidadians earn only $104, and the East Indians a mere $77. Black power advocates claim that they are merely trying to recapture and redirect the resources of the region primarily for the good of the local inhabitants.

The region's black politicans have not taken kindly to the

emergence of the black power groups. The movement is banned entirely in Barbados, St. Lucia, and Grenada, and it is stringently proscribed and persecuted in Jamaica, Trinidad, and Guyana. As a matter of fact, a number of the black power leaders in Trinidad were tried on charges of sedition for the activities of early 1970. Throughout the Caribbean the black population does not demonstrate the minority or marginal qualities that characterize the populations of the United States and Brazil. They form a vertical cross section of the societies. But they are a restive population, largely frozen out of the economic power structure and divided by class distinctions that debilitate the cohesiveness of the societies. While not suffering from racial oppression as much as their fellow blacks in the United States, they nevertheless find that differences of color and class and physical appearance are important in every island or state where the population is racially mixed. What is more, the region will continue to flounder on the periphery of the North American and European (including Russian) spheres of influence—economic, cultural, and political—until they can come together and erase the artificial divisions of language and imperial heritage. There is little hope that any political union will ever take place. The sad experience of the West Indies Federation of the late 1950's and early 1960's will not easily be forgotten. Maybe the politicians will, out of self-interest and self-preservation, realize that they have common problems that may be reduced or eliminated only by cooperative action and rational regional planning. Above all, the people of the Caribbean must be made more aware that they are a predominantly African people who must find the happy synthesis of Africa, America, and Europe, which their culture, population, and interests reflect.

Summary

Across the Americas, group consciousness correlates both with the proportion of Afro-Americans in the population and the relaxation of racial consciousness. Nevertheless, the divisions are not sharp. Instead a gradation exists from the most

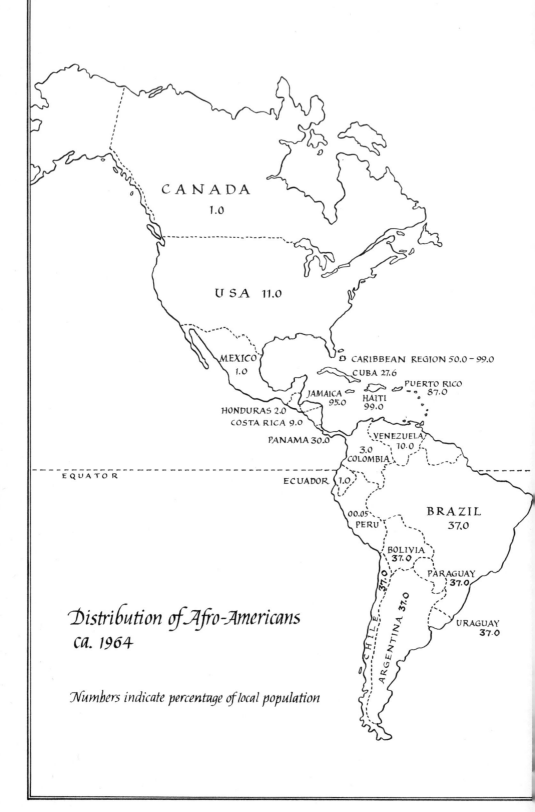

CANADA
1.0

USA 11.0

MEXICO
1.0

CARIBBEAN REGION 50.0 – 99.0

CUBA 27.6

JAMAICA
95.0

PUERTO RICO
87.0

HAITI
99.0

HONDURAS 2.0
COSTA RICA 9.0

PANAMA 30.0

VENEZUELA
10.0

3.0
COLOMBIA

EQUATOR

ECUADOR 1.0

BRAZIL
37.0

00.05
PERU

BOLIVIA
37.0

PARAGUAY
37.0

CHILE 37.0

ARGENTINA 37.0

URAGUAY
37.0

Distribution of Afro-Americans
ca. 1964

Numbers indicate percentage of local population

developed of the settler societies, the United States of America, to the smallest, least developed of the nonsettler societies, English Carriacou. Black consciousness is strongest and most meaningful in the predominantly black independent countries. Political independence and self-confidence of the black masses in the hemisphere, however, mean little in the light of dismal economic and social conditions.

Within settler America, significant differences occur within the United States, as well as between the United States and the other countries. Although the national divisions that led to the Civil War had largely disappeared by the beginning of the twentieth century, the South remains basically similar to what it had been prior to 1860. Racial segregation, although declared illegal, remains in practice. Many black persons continue to view the North as a freer and more egalitarian society. No more integration has occurred in the North, however, and the nation continues to be polarized along racial lines. The large-scale immigration to the northern cities still leaves the majority of the black population in the South. At the same time, it has divided the political potential of this sector of the population. Brazil and Cuba have moved in the opposite direction to the United States. Color and social positions assume more importance than race. In Brazil discrimination is a very subtle affair, and this undermines black civil rights organizations. The state and white society have done very little to either help or hinder the condition of the Afro-Brazilian in the society. Cuba, on the other hand, has taken positive steps since the Castro Revolution to accelerate the social integration of the state, and there the opportunities, position, and acceptance of the black minority are the best in settler America. Puerto Rico, which was a very integrated society at the end of the nineteenth century, has, under the influence of the United States, moved rapidly in the direction of a segregated society. The existence of legislation similar to that in the United States barring discrimination in public places indicates how rapidly the racial situation has deteriorated in that island.

Unlike settler America, the Afro-Americans comprise the majority of the present population of nonsettler America. They do not suffer the same feelings of a minority people, nor do they lack self-confidence. Moreover, they control political power in the recently independent states of the Caribbean (Jamaica, Trinidad and Tobago, Barbados, Guyana), in most of the associated states of the Lesser Antilles, as well as in Haiti, the second oldest republic in the Western Hemisphere. Control of political power, however, has not removed the discrimination based on color, nor has it changed significantly the economic conditions of the predominantly black masses. In most of these countries, therefore, social and economic discontent is common. Some of this has a modified racial slant, aimed both at the governing black elites and the white foreign economic corporations mainly from the United States.

Increased communications with the rest of the world have sharpened the general awareness of race, of fellow Afro-Americans, and of Africans. This heightened consciousness has been partially offset by the political and economic impotence of the black population. Black power advocates in the Caribbean, while a threat to the local ruling elites, are neither as radical nor as insecure as they are in the United States. The fact that their appeal is to the majority of the people gives them greater confidence. They have hope because most Caribbean governments are militarily weak. But so far the West Indian black power groups attempt to force economic socialism rather than to seek political power for themselves. History has not been kind to new small parties in the Caribbean.

Chapter 5

Immigration,
the Afro-Americans,
and Integration

THE RISE OF black consciousness and the problems of race relations, which we discussed in the last chapter, bring us to a new subject. This concerns the relationship of the Afro-Americans with other immigrant groups and the prospects of their integration into the mainstream of American national life. We must begin with the awareness that present American societies are largely the products of immigrants. In most parts of the hemisphere, especially in the core areas of settler and nonsettler America, the indigenous inhabitants form small, scattered, and neglected communities. In those parts of America with a high density of Afro-Americans the majority of immigrants came from Africa. Immigration, therefore, is tied to population composition and Afro-American density pattern. The crucial question then is: What factors determine the absorption of various ethnic groups, particularly the Afro-Americans, into New World societies?

The answer to that question lies in reviewing two kinds of evidence. The first is the nature of immigration. The second is the variables that operate on immigrants. We shall deal with

BRITISH
NORTH AMERICA

Boston 1630

Jamestown 1607

San Diego 1769

VICEROYALTY
OF NEW
SPAIN

Havana 1522

Santo Domingo 1496

Mexico City 1519

Barbados 1625

VICEROYALTY
OF NEW GRANADA

Paramaribo 1640

Cayenne 1626

Quito 1534

EQUATOR

VICEROYALTY
OF NEW
CASTILLE

Pernambuco 1535

Bahia 1549

Lima 1535

BRAZIL

Rio de Janeiro 1565

Valparaiso 1536

VICEROYALTY
OF LA PLATA

Buenos Aires 1536

Portuguese Holdings
Spanish Holdings
English Holdings
French Holdings
1519   Year of Founding Settlement

The Americas: Colonial Holdings
ca. 1770

immigration in the three phases in which it occurred: the conquerors and speculators, the laborers, and the aspiring citizens. The variables that operated were slavery, the structure of American society, and race.

Conquerors, Speculators, and Colonists: 1492–1700

The initial colonization of America was done by fighting men, who were supported by merchants, religious orders, and monarchs. The early settlers came from all over Europe, and they came from every strata of European society: from the nobility, from the towns, from the rural communities. Some came voluntarily or involuntarily to the Americas, and they all adjusted in different ways. Some, like the clergy, continued basically the same occupation that they had in the old country. Many others branched out into other occupations. Some agricultural peasants became great landed proprietors in the Americas and never again tilled the soil by themselves. The Americas offered the opportunity for restructuring the social relations that had prevailed in Europe for centuries. No matter how the bureaucrats and the crown tried to reconstitute the basic structure of Europe in the New World, local differences interfered, and some very significant changes crept into the transplanted models.

One thing was indisputable in the New World: Although the incoming Europeans were a minority, they quickly imposed their system on the lands they entered. A few thousand Spaniards subordinated the people of Mexico and Peru. Similarly, a few thousand Portuguese established the empire in Brazil. A few hundred Englishmen created the New England colonies of North America. This minority set the pattern of the societies that would later develop into different imperial systems throughout the Americas.

The majority of the immigrants who came to the Americas during the first 200 years after the discovery of the new lands were settlers. Whether as fishermen in Newfoundland, farmers in New England, traders in the Dutch Antilles and Brazil, they began to consider America their home. As colonists from Europe, they tried to emulate the social system that they carried with them, making such adjustments as the local environment demanded. They were free men, free to change their living and their place of abode, free to select their families and to exercise their skills.

Indentured Servants and Slaves: 1700–1850

Toward the end of the seventeenth century, however, a change took place. A major reorganization in the products of the colonies demanded more manpower than the steady stream of free persons and indentured inhabitants from Europe could supply. And the reorganization took place when the local American Indian societies were incapable of supplying the nedded labor. Immigration shifted from Europe and became a flood from Africa.

The stream of African immigration to the New World continued until the middle of the nineteenth century and dwarfed all other immigrations at the time. Considering the transportation facilities available at the time, this African immigration was a monumental achievement. Never before had so many persons been removed from their homeland to such a strange environment in such a short time. The transatlantic slave trade, as this form of immigration is known in the history books, was a unique experience in the history of the world.

The early Europeans had come largely as individuals, but they had come into a society in which they either fitted or controlled. This was not so for the millions of Africans. Their transfer to the Americas created severe strains on both the African and American societies. African immigrants to the Americas came involuntarily and fitted in at the lowest social, political, and economic levels.

In an earlier chapter we examined the African slave contribution to the Americas and we looked at the effect of slavery on the various societies of the Americas. The African experience in the Americas was unique. The Africans were the only ones who came as slaves. Certainly others came in some form of servitude. Some early Europeans—the English indentured servants, the French *engagés,* or the Portuguese *degredados*—came to serve the "respectable" colonists who had migrated under their own initiative. Their service was for a period of time, and they were drawn from the same basic stock of their fellow colonists. As soon as their period of enforced servitude expired, they assumed their positions as free and equal citizens in the country, if they so desired. Moreover, they were a minority of the population, and they could be easily assimilated into the mainstream of the colony's life and existence. As slaves, the Africans were condemned to a lifetime tenure, from which escape was infrequent and unusual. Moreover, the slave was the lowest social being in the colony—just as the plantation worker, or "coolie," became the lowest in status in the postslavery societies of the New World.

Even when the slave escaped from his slavery, he was never free to assume an equal place in the society of which he was a part. He was alien in culture, often in speech, and certainly in physical appearance of phenotype. This phenotypical distinction was to plague the persons of African descent all through the history of the peoples of the New World, and it remains the most difficult barrier to the acceptance and assimilation of the Afro-American population.

All Africans came to the New World as individuals rather than as members of a corporate group. Besides, the immigrants were predominantly male. This made it far more difficult for the African to maintain a cohesive and vital culture, representative of any part of Africa. African society in the Americas, therefore, was really a hodgepodge of African elements, a broad representation of the varied groups from which the slaves were drawn. Most of these social characteristics were West African, but they were not identifiably West African as, say, the use of spaghetti in Argentina is identifiably Italian. When the Africans escaped to form their separate society, it was a compromise of African and American characteristics. Circumstances made social reconstruction along the lines of the European society—which was often their greatest common denominator—and forced the Afro-Americans to use a European language as their *lingua franca.* All other immigrants formed sufficiently cohesive groups, and so their culture was not as disastrously destroyed as that of the African. If these groups therefore tended to become American, this represented, unlike the position of the African, a more conscious choice.

National Groups: 1850–1950

The third wave of immigrants came between the end of the nineteenth century and the middle of the twentieth century. These were national groups, drawn from recognized European nation-states. Unlike the earlier African migration, the sexual balance was greater among these immigrants. They came voluntarily in groups rather than as individuals. Indeed, variety and sexual balance were the distinguishing features of the so-called "new immigration" between 1880 and 1924, when the United States adopted a quota system of immigration.

The newer immigrants came from diverse countries including Bohemia, Finland, France, Germany, Great Britain, Holland, Ireland, Italy, Norway, Poland, Portugal, Sweden, and Syria. Some of these countries, such as Ireland, Great Britain, and Germany, had been long and steady exporters of people to the United States. Others, such as the Italians, the Bohemians, and the diverse nationalities who contributed the Jews, were recent immigrants in the limited sense that they had only begun to arrive in large numbers. These immigrants came largely as complete families, or at least sexually balanced. In any case, the sexual balance among the immigrants was better than that of the early explorers and settlers, as well as the Africans.

Given any form of migration, it is usual for the males to outnumber the females. This had been true throughout the history of immigration until the modern times, and it probably holds true for all current migrations, except the Irish, Italians, and the current migration of West Indian domestics to Canada. But the Italian sexual imbalance adjusted itself as the relatives of the earlier immigrants came over after 1900 to join the first wave. The proportions given in Table 5 do not reflect the reality of the Italian situation, but later figures are difficult to obtain.

TABLE 5   *Immigrants to U.S.A., 1899–1909*

Group	Percentage of Males	Percentage of Females
Irish	48.0	52.0
Hebrew	56.0	44.0
French	59.0	41.0
Portuguese	59.0	41.0
German	59.0	41.0
Scandinavian	61.0	39.0
British	61.0	39.0
Syrian	70.0	30.0
Polish and other Eastern Europeans	70.0	30.0
Italians (1895–99)	75.0	25.0

Because these immigrants came mainly as family units, their accommodation to the new life was easier. This pattern was true, whether these immigrations went to Canada, the United States, Mexico, Brazil, or Argentina.

The Assimilation of Immigrant Groups

There are three distinct differences among the three phases of immigration to the Americas. The first phase of distinctly European immigrants established the pattern of later American society. The second phase, coming from Africa as slaves, fitted into the pattern of American society that the first wave of immigrants had designed. Special laws had to be designed in the various American societies to govern the African immigrants, since the societies in general subscribed to European laws that had little or no relevance to the slave society. In the final phase the immigrants conformed to the general pattern of society, but they had no legal distinctions as slaves. Little communities of Germans existed in southern Brazil, or of Italians in Buenos Aires and Entre Rios in Argentina. But the newcomers tried to speak the language of the host country, and they tried to conform to the laws that prevailed. To a great degree, therefore, these third-phase immigrants consciously sought integration, although some were pressured into integrating into the societies that they found in the New World.

Nowhere in the Americas did total integration occur. Nowhere was the process of integrating a large number of immigrants easy. The newly arrived third-phase immigrants formed microscopic enclaves of their culture and nationality in the various countries. Often these were in the larger cities, where opportunities for industrial labor or commercial activity were greatest. Despite the overriding desire on the part of most European immigrants at the end of the last century to engage in agriculture, by the time that most of them were settled in the New World the opportunities for agricultural pursuit were no longer feasible, or rewarding enough. At the beginning of the twentieth century, the rapid industrialization of countries such as Canada, the United States, and southern Brazil and the political manipulations of the landed cattlement, or *estancieros*, of Argentina had reduced the opportunities for landholding considerably, but these had opened great prospects in the industrial field. Although essentially an agricultural and rural people, the later immigrants, therefore, settled down to the ghetto life of the cities and the repetitious, but sometimes skilled, jobs of the factories. Asians and Africans formed the only two groups of people to be legally excluded by name and national origin from the United States. The Chinese have traveled far along the road of national integration into the American way of life. The Afro-American is farthest behind in getting full political rights, economic equality, and social acceptance. Integration into the mainstream of American life depends on the position that any group bears in relation to the national norm. In the United States this norm is represented by the white Anglo-Saxon. In Brazil, the Portuguese hold the highest position; and the Spanish-speaking Creole in Spanish America. Settler groups, or their derivatives, form the norm throughout the Americas, even in the predominantly Afro-American islands of the Caribbean.

Problems of Afro-American Integration

The real difficulties in integrating the Afro-American population into the national system, politically, economically and socially, are threefold. The first is, of course, the history of slavery and its effects on the nation. The second is the structure of American society, which operates as a coalition of interests rather than as a unified system. The third is race. These difficulties are most evident in the United States of America.

The process of black immigration to the United States, as to any other country, prohibited the formation of a cohesive black social or cultural unit. The conditions of the slave society further denigrated and subordinated the black population. They were ruthlessly exploited as workers, and they were never accepted as a valuable part of the society. After the abolition of slavery, the black population as a group was incapable of competing with the newly arrived European immigrants. Moreover, they were legally, socially, and physically excluded from an ever-increasing number of occupations and opportunities for individual advancement. They had little education, little money, and virtually no land. What is more, the legacy of their enslavement had been the virtual destruction of their self-confidence.

Nevertheless, despite what individual black Americans may declare, as a group they are a part of the North American cultural system. That is undeniable. In terms of language, tastes, aspirations, and conduct, they are closer to the national norms of the United States than to any other country in the world. Of course, no nation or culture is homogeneous. Each nation is a regional coalition and has ethnic varieties. This variety is recognized as an intrinsic part of any dynamic society: It is part of the folk culture. This process of integration has been very slow in the United States. The traditions of slavery still form a recognizable part of the present social conduct. If the country is to endure as a strong and unified nation, major efforts must be exerted to bridge the gap between the races and between the majority and the minority. These efforts, however, can only succeed if the American society becomes more democratic.

Equal education and equal opportunity can, with equal legal recognition, go far toward the assimilation of the black minority in the United States. Even then, there exists another problem: the political structure of the society. In the United States, political power gravitates to those who command the votes, those who have powerful lobbies, and those who have effective representation in Congress. Congress is where particular interests resolve their differences. Private, public, and regional interests come together there to work out satisfactory compromises. There labor, capital, industry, and other ethnic groups all have their chief spokesmen. The blacks, however, have little or no political power in Congress, and they do not form a prominent interest group. They form no part of the collective voice of labor, since they are virtually excluded from the labor unions. They have no voice in the big industries such as oil, coal, steel, and motor engineering, since the black people neither own these concerns nor have substantial interests there. They form a negligible proportion of the farmers and, therefore, have no effective voice in the farm lobby. The population is so scattered across the country that their combined vote in a presidential election is less effective than their voting proportion of the electorate. While they may affect electoral results in states such as Illinois, and probably Ohio, they really cannot directly influence the outcome of any election. Indeed, it is still possible for a major presidential candidate to win an election on the federal level without the support of the so-called "black vote."

Given the present political structure, therefore, the blacks are relatively impotent. Without the necessary political power, they cannot win the political concessions that have enabled some other minority groups to escape from the burden of their position. In the final analysis, of course, the government will have to realize that social justice demands that the good of the minority is inseparable from the good of the entire group. The black population can and ought to contribute to the nation in all respects. But they can only do so if they share the constitutional guarantees, the opportunities, the training, and the self-confidence that pertain to every responsible citizen. Good training offers the chance of better jobs. Better jobs mean a better family structure and a better opportunity for the offspring to fit into the society, paying the taxes, buying the products, and exercising the judgment of every conscientious citizen. The quality of a country depends upon the quality of its citizenry, and good citizens begin with a good education and the ability to make intelligent evaluations. No alienated group can ever exercise the functions of a citizen. Besides, every alienated group is a potentially revolutionary element in a state.

Nevertheless, the society needs more than mere legal changes in education and more jobs for the blacks. The nation needs to be less exclusive in its cultural values. Race and color have been the major handicaps to the integration of the Afro-American into the society. All the other immigrant groups—Jews, Italians, Polish, Albanians, Swedish, British, Greeks, and Lithuanians—especially those of the later nineteenth and early twentieth centuries, experienced some degree of discrimination, prejudice, and *de facto* segregation. Nevertheless, they had one saving factor: They were, to a greater or lesser degree of recognition, "white." It is possible to argue that all these groups possess a special distinguishing physical appearance that is basically similar and often indistinguishable to nonmembers of the group. The Afro-American, however, has a distinctive basic appearance. This sets him apart and makes it impossible for him to merge as an individual into the larger society in the same way that European-derived immigrants have been able to do.

Race and color are distinctions, but they should be no handicaps. It is possible for the society to neutralize the effects of race and color. It requires a social environment in which negative values are not placed upon these characteristics. Indeed, experiments show that young children are quite devoid of qualitative color and race distinctions. As they grow up, society instills in them the biases and discriminatory sense that they reflect in their adult lives.

One tragedy of American education is the way in which segregation and discrimination have adversely affected general school textbooks. School-age children are denied the opportunity to appreciate the variety and complexity of their history, especially the fact that their roots as a nation join Europe, Africa, and native America. Good books would enable black children *before* they attend college to discover that they also have some heroes. Black-studies courses offered in colleges are a highly inadequate method of correcting the prevailing biases of the society because they affect too few persons too late in their lives.

On the other hand, white children should never assume, based on their reading and general knowledge, that the blacks were either absent or minimal in the evolution of their national history. American textbooks, therefore, are both a liability to education and to scientific inquiry. They are, however, the products of a mutually reinforcing cleavage society, where even the myths are designed to strengthen the white sector and exclude, weaken, and undermine the nonwhite.

The unilateral subordination and negation of the Afro-American sector does not occur in either the Caribbean or the Brazilian society. For both in Brazil and in the Caribbean countries, social cleavages are cross-cutting, involving all races and colors. Africans and Afro-Americans have been a recognized and accepted part of the national tradition. Black men have participated in politics, the arts, war, the economy, and every facet of the society with distinction equal to any other group. Of course, the societies are predominantly black in the Caribbean and about one-third black in Brazil. There is, therefore, a numerical difference, which is reflected in social action.

The crucial difference between the modern United States, on the one hand, and the Caribbean states and Brazil, on the other, is that high social status is denied the black person in the United States, while it is possible elsewhere. The Afro-American population in the United States suffers more from social exclusion than from economic exclusion. For this reason, the Afro-American in the United States might be in a better economic position, in terms of per capita income, than the majority of the population of any other country in the hemisphere with the exception of Canada. In any case, the average per capita income of the Afro-American in the United States of America far exceeds that of his contemporary elsewhere in the hemisphere. Nevertheless, the possibility of upward social mobility, of attaining the highest stratum of the society, is next to impossible in the United States.

Conversely, the Afro-American is fully integrated into the social structure of Caribbean society. There, however, the Afro-American population is excluded from significant participation in the economic sphere. The Caribbean countries have all continued the traditional pattern of economic activities oriented toward the North Atlantic and Russian economic systems. The local economies, therefore, are controlled by foreigners or their representatives. In either case, not enough benefits for economic development remain in the region for the majority of the population. For this reason, black power in the Caribbean is not just a narrow ethnic slogan designed to foster cohesion among the black population. It means tangible economic participation of the lower orders of society, which in Jamaica, Martinique, Trinidad, Guyana, and Honduras include non–Afro-American elements. Lack of local economic opportunities forces large numbers of West Indians to emigrate each year.

The Brazilian situation differs in that the Afro-American populations have not yet achieved the degree of social and political control that they have in the Caribbean. Their economic plight, however, is the same.

Another way of seeing the general situation is that the social, economic, and political divisions in the Caribbean tend to be vertical, while in Brazil and the United States they tend to be horizontal. A socially vertical subdivision gravitates toward greater integration, since it includes all ethnic groups. Horizontal subdivisions facilitate exclusion and foster prejudice, discrimination, and segregation. But a vertically stratified society results only from a rough equality of opportunity that allows each individual to succeed or fail, regardless of the motivation of the group. A socially healthy society is one in which the price of individuality is not so great that men find it better to conform to the group.

Summary

Of all the immigrant groups to the Americas, only the Africans came involuntarily. Moreover, on their entry to American colonial society, they were distributed, subordinated, specially distinguished as slaves, and largely denied the opportunities to retain and develop their indigenous culture.

In continental America, where the settler society prevailed, the Afro-American population remained a minority. Color, occupation, custom, and law combined to form the mutually reinforcing distinctions that considerably inhibited the mobility of the nonwhite group.

In Brazil and the Caribbean, the greater number of black persons in the society permitted their greater mobility and social acceptance. As a majority of the postslavery Caribbean population, the blacks had a greater impact on the creole society and a lesser feeling of inferiority and insecurity.

Chapter 6

Conclusion

The previous chapters reviewed a number of questions deal-ing with the social and political integration of the Afro-American population into the national states of the Western Hemisphere. All along we have simplified and separated a very complex pattern. Nevertheless, we can now conclude that five major factors influenced this pattern during the course of its evolution (see Table 6, page 132):

1. The original settler or nonsettler nature of colonization and development of the region
2. The system of slavery and the impact that it had on the local society
3. The Afro-American population density that prevailed both during and after slavery
4. The social structure and attitudes that developed as the society matured in each region
5. The phases of immigration by which this Afro-American population came to be a part of the American social sys-tem

The uneven operation of these factors over a period of time

TABLE 6 *Factors Affecting Afro-American Integration*

Factor	U.S.A.	The Caribbean	Latin America
1. Colonial type	Settler	Nonsettler	Settler
2. Slave system	Medium holdings, with tendency toward individually owned. Groups in excess of 100 very rare. Society not determined by plantation.	Large holdings in excess of 100 frequent. Plantations dominate social structure. Spanish islands with significant urban base.	With exception of Brazil, large holdings rare. Parts of Brazil conform to Caribbean pattern.
3. Population density	Greatest concentration in the South, with urban increase in North after slavery. In general, less than 10 percent of the population.	Dense throughout the region during and after slavery. Range: 30–95 percent of the population.	Dense only in some parts of Brazil. About 40 percent in Brazil, negligible in Argentina, Andean region, and Mexico.
4. Phase of immigration	As slaves during the second phase of immigration. Very few admitted during the national period of high immigration, 1820–1924.	Peak Afro-American immigration as slaves, but unlike U.S.A., the newcomers consistently outnumbered the American-born sector of the population.	Brazil similar to the Caribbean. Volume to Brazil extremely high.
5. Social structure and integration	Society autonomous and exclusively white-oriented. Sharp divisions between black and white. Miscegenation not accepted. Afro-American integration low.	Value systems oriented toward Europe, and societies appendages of European metropolises. But the reality of a three-tiered society recognized in law and custom, with distinctions between white, free person of color, and black. Mobility relatively fluid within the color-caste distinctions; far less so across the lines. With miscegenation a way of life, and a declining white elite, integration high.	

produced the variations in the national societies that we find in the Americas today.

The principal difference between settler and nonsettler America stemmed from the attitudes of the early colonists either to form permanent reproductions of the mother country in the New World or to have temporary places of exploitation. In these temporary areas, the overriding considerations were to make a fortune and return to participate in the society of the homeland. The European-American element of nonsettler America, unlike settler America, suffered from a scarcity of European women and a vulnerability to the economic, political, and intellectual conditions of Europe. Settler America, therefore unlike nonsettler America, began and continued as a complete social unit, free to mature by itself. Like all societies with contact with others, it was influenced from the outside, but crucial decisions affecting the society were made within it, not forced upon it by others.

The main settler societies were either in the temperate regions, such as Argentina, southern Brazil, the United States of America, and Canada, or in the highland tropical regions, which came close to being temperate, such as in Peru, Mexico, and the highland region of Colombia and Venezuela. The different societies that developed in these areas owed a lot to the type of settlers who came from Europe to form them. Iberians of the early sixteenth century tended to be more religious and more observant of the medieval traditions of their homeland. English and French settlers of the seventeenth century had lost most of these medieval traditions in their homeland, tended to be less religious, and to be more from the urban lower classes and merchants.

The system of slavery, and the impact that it had on local society, stemmed from the needs of either settler or nonsettler America. Settlers tended to need a lower number of slaves, with many of them used in domestic services. Nonsettlers required much more labor and used slaves in large numbers, usually in gangs. The systems of slavery fell, not according to the European background of the region, but according to whether the slaves were held essentially as individuals or as large groups of laborers. These two patterns coincide with the settler and nonsettler types of American society. Neither the systems of slavery nor the types of society were found in a "pure" or undiluted form. Societies existed in varying combinations of these two types and systems. This was especially true for the plantation slave society, which spanned both settler and nonsettler America, although it was most pronounced in the tropical regions of nonsettler America. The plantation slave society was the largest importer of slaves into the Americas, except in the southern United States.

The slave society was a unique experience for Europeans in the New World. Eventually it permeated every facet of European economic, political, and social life in the hemisphere. It led to the identification and subordination of the African in American society, first as a slave, and then as a free person. After slavery, this identification and subordination led to various forms of exclusion. Some, such as in the United States of America, had some legal support. Elsewhere, while no legal distinctions were made between Afro-American and other sectors of the society, custom and circumstances operated to hinder the rapid integration of the Afro-American.

These customs and circumstances followed the pattern of population density in the Americas. In a hemispheric overview, the present population density follows closely the involvement of the regions in slavery and the slave trade. Very roughly, tropical America imported more slaves and its present population reflects the African influence. Nevertheless, to say that nearly 70 percent of Afro-Americans today live within the tropics is to place a geographical emphasis that grossly distorts both the history of Afro-American life in the New World and the reality of contemporary Afro-American participation in the national societies.

The continental United States of America, which falls outside the tropics, has nearly 31 percent of all the Afro-Americans in the New World. Since this region imported less than 5 percent of the Africans who came to the Americas, the region stands unique as an area of Afro-American fertility and reproduction. Within the context of national life in the United States, however, Afro-Americans comprise a mere 10 percent of the population and have a minimal impact on political life. On the other hand, in some countries in the Caribbean, Afro-Americans form the overwhelming majority of the population and dominate the political life. The most important observation about the pattern of Afro-American population density is that it is greater in nonsettler America than in settler America.

The local Afro-American population affects both the structure of the society and the attitudes toward that sector. Attitudes are affected by policital decisions, and political decisions are made within the framework of the national state. When we come to talk of local attitudes toward the Afro-American and his integration into society, we must look less at the larger divisions of settler and nonsettler America than at the smaller divisions of nation-states. Where Afro-Americans form a majority of the population, and where they have political power, race seems to be a less important consideration than color, social status, and economic position. This is the meaning of the Brazilian and Caribbean phrase "money whitens." Unfortunately, Afro-Americans do not control the national economies anywhere in the Americas. Even in countries that are politically independent, the major industries and the main sources of money and wealth are either owned or controlled by Europeans or white Americans. The lack of control over the resources and economies of these countries seriously undermines the ability of the governments to ameliorate the general condition of that part of the population still in poverty. Poverty and unemployment and a limited opportunity for education and other social services characterize the Afro-American population wherever they may be found.

In the Caribbean and Latin America, however, Afro-Americans form a part of all the social strata. Afro-Americans, therefore, share every occupation and every status—even though they predominate in low-skilled, low-paying jobs. These societies, therefore, are not structured along racial lines that exclude any particular group. They are socially democratic or societies of mutually cross-cutting cleavages. The pace of integration therefore tends to increase as the Afro-Americans move out of poverty and into the mainstream of the society. In Latin America the Afro-Americans form only a part of the underprivileged groups. Race had less biological significance than it did in the United States of

America, and so it is referred to as "notional race." People are classified by physical appearance or social pattern rather than by blood or ancestors. On the other hand, classification by blood and deliberate legal exclusion, as occur in the United States, create a rigidity and reluctance that greatly inhibit the opportunities for integration of the Afro-American population. The United States is therefore a mutually reinforcing cleavage society. The mutually reinforcing nature of society in the United States separates that society from the other settler societies and gives to that country the peculiarity that we have noted there throughout this book. Social attitudes reflect the reality of social conditions.

These social attitudes, in turn, affected the acceptance of immigrant groups to the Americas. Afro-Americans were the only immigrant group to be distinguished by color rather than national origin. In the United States of America, where they form a minority group, they came at a time when the society thought strongly and negatively about Africans and slavery. Not only were Afro-Americans distinguishable from the rest of the population, they were also deliberately segregated and downgraded. Other immigrant minorities, on the other hand, were not easily distinguishable and were not deliberately excluded from the society. As national groups and as complete social entities, sexually balanced, and culturally self-conscious, they adapted to the American way of life without difficulties. African immigrants, as sexually imbalanced and reluctant immigrants to the New World, found it much harder to retain or develop a vital culture that would reinforce their self-confidence. In the Americas they were forced to make hasty and *ad hoc* accommodations to their American conditions. African immigrants, therefore, had peculiar disadvantages, which the other immigrant groups to the New World did not have.

Across the Americas, the Afro-Americans have encountered a series of conditions that have wittingly and unwittingly served to identify and handicap the development of this group. These conditions vary, and have always varied, from place to place. Nowhere, however, have they combined with the adverse effect found in the United States of America. The Afro-American population is least integrated in the United States for this reason.

Suggested Readings

Introductory Reading Material

THE GENERAL READER who wants to expand his information and understanding of the American slave systems should begin with the secondary authorities that treat the subject in a rather broad way. Many of the best works are available in relatively inexpensive paperback editions. The best general work about slave systems in the United States is the reliable and highly readable narrative of John Hope Franklin: *From Slavery to Freedom: A History of Negro Americans* (New York: Knopf, 1967),* which examines the Afro-American dimension of the United States until the end of the 1960's and has a very good bibliography. The Portuguese slave systems are studied in the short book by C. R. Boxer: *Race Relations in the Portuguese Colonial Empire 1415–1825* (London: Oxford University Press, 1963). This should be supplemented for the later period in Brazil by Robert Brent Toplin: *The Abolition of Slavery in Brazil* (New York: Atheneum, 1972), which describes the relations between masters and slaves during the nineteenth century and meticulously analyzes the forces that led to the collapse of the

Note: An asterisk indicates that the book is available in a paperback edition.

Brazilian slave system. There is no adequate single volume for the Spanish American system. John V. Lombardi: *The Decline and Abolition of Negro Slavery in Venezuela, 1820–1854* (Westport, Conn.: Greenwood Publishing, 1971) is valuable for its painstaking research into the nature of slavery and the uses to which slaves were put in a system that did not fully experience the plantation system of agriculture. The arguments put forward by Lombardi sharply modify the views given in Frank Tannenbaum: *Slave and Citizen: The Negro in the Americas* (New York: Knopf, 1947),* which attempts to establish differences among the American slave systems by emphasizing the Iberian legacies of benevolent paternalism and corporate responsibility by the Roman Catholic Church and the imperial bureaucracy. J. H. Parry and P. M. Sherlock: *A Short History of the West Indies* (New ed., New York: St. Martin's Press, 1968)* gives a full description of the English Caribbean system, tracing the process from its initiation to its decline.

The thorough examination given by Philip D. Curtin: *The Atlantic Slave Trade, A Census* (Madison: University of Wisconsin Press, 1969)* carefully scrutinizes the subject and is far more detailed than the modest title suggests. Curtin measures the flow of the slave trade through the centuries and suggests the implications for the development of American societies at each stage. It is a vital book on the subject.

The implications of race and the legal, social, and psychological conflicts of the slave society emerge strongly in Philip D. Curtin: *Two Jamaicas: The Role of Ideas in a Tropical Colony, 1830–1865* (New York: Atheneum, 1968).* The conflicts arising from the peculiar situation of the Jamaican whites during the nineteenth century can be extended to all the white groups living in the exploitation colonies after the beginning of the eighteenth century, regardless of metropolitan origin. M. Mörner: *Race Mixture in the History of Latin America* (Boston: Little, Brown, 1967)* studies the historical evolution of the problem of miscegenation in the Spanish American empire and accentuates the inconsistency of the Spanish in dealing with race and color. P. Mason: *Race Relations* (New York: Oxford University Press, 1971)* projects the problems on a universal plane and suggests that race relations are a matter of perception and can be modified by conscious action; but the various articles in J. H. Franklin, ed., *Color and Race* (Boston: Beacon Press, 1968)* diminish the optimism that such change can easily be accomplished.

David Cohen and Jack P. Greene, eds., *Neither Slave nor Free: The Freedmen of African descent in the slave societies of the New World* (Baltimore: Johns Hopkins University Press, 1972) brings together ten studies on the intermediate group of free nonwhite persons in the slave societies in Cuba, Barbados, Brazil, Jamaica, St. Domingue, Surinam, Curaçao, colonial Spanish America, and the United States. Some of the articles are of exceptional quality and provide more detailed information than can be gathered from other studies dealing peripherally with the same theme, such as Marvin Harris: *Patterns of Race in the Americas* (New York: Walker, 1964)* and the prize-winning book by Carl Degler: *Neither Black nor White: Slavery and Race Relations in Brazil and the United States* (New York: Macmillan, 1971).*

The collections of selected readings by Laura Foner and Eugene Genovese, eds., *Slavery in the New World* (Englewood Cliffs, N.J.: Prentice-Hall, 1969)* and A. Weinstein and O. Gatell, eds., *American Negro Slavery* (New York: Oxford, 1968),* while excellent, require that the reader have some background information for optimal absorption. Nevertheless, they do provide a good source for some stimulating excerpts.

Additional Bibliographical Notes

The more informed reader will find that for most of tropical America, the institution and experience of slavery have received considerable attention, especially from social historians. Although the majority of the studies are still conducted at the national and local level, the quality of scholarship improves as the quantity increases. For studies of the United States, the place to begin is still with the highly readable narrative of John Hope Franklin: *From Slavery to Freedom* (New York: Knopf, 1967), which gives the broad overview. Kenneth M. Stampp: *The Peculiar Institution*

(New York: Knopf, 1956) began a radical swing away from the apologetic, paternalistic view that had long prevailed among historians concerned with the South. Richard C. Wade: *Slavery in the Cities: The South, 1820–1860* (New York: Oxford University Press, 1964) accentuates the wide differences between the rural and urban forms of slavery. Robert Starobin: *Industrial Slavery in the Old South* (New York: Oxford University Press, 1970) examines the use of slaves in southern industries between 1790 and 1860 and reveals a great deal about race relations before the Civil War. Eugene D. Genovese: *The Political Economy of Slavery* (New York: Pantheon, 1965) sees slavery as an integral part of the social system in the South, which led to incompatibility with the capitalistic North. Some excellent essays have been brought together in L. Foner and E. Genovese, eds.: *Slavery in the New World: A Reader in Comparative History* (Englewood Cliffs, N.J.: Prentice-Hall, 1969); I. Unger and D. Reimers, eds.: *The Slavery Experience in the United States* (New York: Holt, Rinehart and Winston, 1970); and A. Weinstein and F. O. Gatell: *American Negro Slavery* (New York: Oxford University Press, 1968). J. H. Parry and P. M. Sherlock: *A Short History of the West Indies* (3rd. ed., New York: St. Martin's Press, 1971) gives a concise, general view of developments in the Caribbean region. A growing list of high-quality monographs provides deeper insights into individual islands. For Cuba, read M. Moreno Fraginals: *El Ingenio* (Havana: Unesco, 1964); H. Aimes: *A History of Slavery in Cuba* (New York: Putnam's Sons, 1907); R. Cepero Bonilla: *Azucar y Abolición* (Havana: Instituto de Historia, 1948); F. Knight: *Slave Society in Cuba During the Nineteenth Century* (Madison: University of Wisconsin Press, 1970). For Puerto Rico, L. Diaz Soler: *Historia de la Esclavitud Negra en Puerto Rico* (Rio Piedras: University of Puerto Rico Press, 1965); S. Mintz, "The Role of Forced Labor in Nineteenth Century Puerto Rico," in *Caribbean Historical Review*, 2 (1951), 134–141. For Jamaica, Orlando Patterson: *The Sociology of Slavery* (London: MacGibbon & Kee, 1967), which has a useful index on slave imports and exports from that island; and Edward Braithwaite: *The Development of Creole Society in Jamaica, 1770–1820* (Oxford: Clarendon

Press, 1971), which gives excellent details of the slave structure. For the eastern islands, E. Goveia: *Slave Society in the British Leeward Islands at the End of the Eighteenth Century* (New Haven: Yale University Press, 1965); and L. J. Ragatz: *The Fall of the Planter Class in the British Caribbean, 1763–1833* (New York: Century, 1928). For the French Caribbean, read Gaston Martin: *Histoire de l'esclavage dans les colonies françaises* (Paris: Presses Universitaires de France, 1948); and C. L. R. James: *The Black Jacobins* (New ed., New York; Vintage, 1966), which, although it emphasizes the revolution in St. Domingue, provides very valuable background material. Also useful is Gwendolyn M. Hall: *Social Control in Slave Plantation Societies: A comparison of St. Dominque and Cuba* (Baltimore: Johns Hopkins University Press, 1971).

For slavery in Brazil, begin with the lyrical, though misleading Gilberto Freyre: *The Mansions and the Shanties* (New York: Knopf, 1963); Emilia Viotti da Costa: *Da Senzala a Colonia* (São Paulo: Universidade de São Paulo, 1966); João Dornas Filho: *A escravidão no Brasil* (Rio de Janeiro: Civilização Brasileira, S. A., 1939: A. Ramos: *The Negro in Brazil* (Washington: Assoc. Publishers, 1939). Stanley Stein: *Vassouras: A Brazilian Coffee Country, 1850–1890* (New York: Atheneum, 1970) and Robert Conrad: *The Destruction of Brazilian Slavery, 1850–1888* (Berkeley and Los Angeles: University of California Press, 1972) are excellent for the nineteenth century. Valuable information is found in a number of general works, including R. E. Poppino: *Brazil* (New York: Oxford University Press, 1970) and Caio Prado, Jr.: *The Colonial Background of Modern Brazil* (Berkeley and Los Angeles: University of California Press, 1969).

The literature on slavery in continental Spanish America is much less prolific than for Brazil, since Africans did not play a fundamental role in the national and social development. R. Mellafe: *La esclavitud en Hispanoamérica* (Buenos Aires: Editorial Universitaria, 1964) gives a very brief but fairly reliable summary. Regional emphasis can be added by reading G. Aguirre Beltran: *La población negra de Mexico, 1519–1810* (Mexico: Fonda de Cultura Económica, 1946); David M. Davidson: "Negro Slave Control and Resistance in Colonial

Mexico, 1519–1650," in *Hispanic American Historical Review*, 46 (1966), 235–353; John V. Lombardi: *The Decline and Abolition of Negro Slavery in Venezuela, 1820–1854* (Westport, Conn.: Greenwood Publishing Corp., 1971); J. Lockhart: *Spanish Peru, 1532–1560* (Madison: University of Wisconsin Press, 1968).

Even though eminent ex-slaves, such as Frederick Douglass in the United States and Juan Manzano in Cuba, have published in prose and verse their impressions of slavery during the nineteenth century, the general reactions of the slaves to slavery have been neglected in the literature. This is now being rectified. For some "views from below," see Esteban Montejo: *The Autobiography of a Runaway Slave,* edited by Miguel Barnet (New York: Random House, 1968), which is interesting, though not as useful as it might have been had not Montejo lived most of his adolescent life as a hermit; and Norman R. Yetman: *Life Under the "Peculiar Institution":* *Selections from the Slave Narrative Collection* (New York: Holt, Rinehart and Winston, 1970); George P. Rawick: *The American Slave: A Composite Autobiography. From Sundown to Sunup. The Making of the Black Community* (Westport, Conn.: Greenwood Publishing Corp., 1972).

Stanley Elkins: *Slavery: A Problem in American Institutional and Intellectual Life* (Chicago: University of Chicago Press, 1959) is an intellectual tour de force that handles the problem in a far less authoritative way than Gunnar Myrdal: *An American Dilemma* (New York: Harper, 1944). Frank Tannenbaum: *Slave and Citizen* (New York: Knopf, 1947) stimulated the comparative approach. His thesis has been supported, revised, refuted, or refined by a number of scholars, including H. Klein: *Slavery in the Americas* (Chicago: University of Chicago Press, 1967), which compares Cuba and Virginia; D. B. Davis: *The Problem of Slavery in Western Culture* (Ithaca: Cornell University Press, 1966), the beginning of a projected multivolume examination of the entire problem through time and space; E. D. Genovese: *The World the Slaveholders Made* (New York: Pantheon, 1969), a masterly essay in comparative history, which will be a standard reference for a very long time. The economic ramifications are dealt with in E. Williams: *Capitalism and Slavery*

(Chapel Hill: University of North Carolina Press, 1944); Celso Furtado: *The Economic Growth of Brazil* (Berkeley and Los Angeles: University of California Press, 1963); Manuel Moreno Fraginals: *El Ingenio* (Havana: Unesco, 1964); Roland T. Ely: *Cuando Reinaba su majestad el azúcar* (Buenos Aires: Editorial Sudamericana, 1963); Raul Cepero Bonilla: *Obras históricas* (Havana: Instituto de Historia, 1963); and E. Genovese: *The Political Economy of Slavery* (New York: Pantheon, 1965).

The literature on the slave trade is abundant, both generally and regionally. Philip D. Curtin's *The Atlantic Slave Trade: A Census* (Madison: University of Wisconsin Press, 1969) is by far the best single book to date. B. Davidson: *Black Mother: The Years of the African Slave Trade* (Boston: Little, Brown, 1961) and Daniel Mannix and Malcom Cowley: *Black Cargoes: A History of the Atlantic Slave Trade* (New York: Viking, 1962) remain highly readable, if not entirely reliable.

Race relations are dealt with by most of the authors concerned with slavery; of particular merit are W. Jordan: *White Over Black American Attitudes to the Negro, 1550–1812* (Chapel Hill: University of North Carolina Press, 1968); C. R. Boxer: *Race Relations in the Portuguese Colonial Empire, 1415–1825* (Oxford: Oxford University Press, 1963); M. Mörner: *Race Mixture in the History of Latin America* (Boston; Little, Brown, 1967); H. Hoetink: *Caribbean Race Relations: A Study of Two Variants* (London: Oxford University Press, 1967); M. Harris: *Patterns of Race in the Americas* (New York: Walker, 1964). The complexity of attitudes, their genesis and perpetuation, can be studied in M. Herskovits: *The Myth of the Negro Past* (New ed., Boston, Beacon Press, 1958); P. D. Curtin: *The Image of Africa* (Madison: University of Wisconsin Press, 1964); G. W. Allport, *The Nature of Prejudice* (New York: Doubleday, 1954); W. Stanton: *The Leopard's Spots* (Chicago: University of Chicago Press, 1960); P. van den Berghe: *Race and Racism: A Comparative Perspective* (New York: Wiley, 1967); and the stimulating collection of essays in J. H. Franklin, ed.: *Color and Race* (Boston: Little, Brown 1968). The peculiar enigmas of Brazil are handled in F. Fernandez and R. Bastide, eds.: *Brancos e negros em São Paulo* (2nd ed., São Paulo: Companhia Editora Nacional, 1959); F. Henrique Cardoso and Octavio Ianni: *Cor e mobilidade social em Florianopolis* (São Paulo: Companhia Editora Nacional, 1960); and Thales de Azevedo: *Cultura e situacão racial no Brasil* (Rio de Janeiro: Civilização Brasileira, S.A. 1966). Carl N. Degler: *Neither Black nor White* (New York: Macmillan, 1971) compares both the Brazilian and United States history of slavery and race relations. Insights into the positive as well as negative aspects of racial integration can be derived from O. Handlin: *Race and Nationality in American Life* (Boston: Beacon Press, 1950); P. Mason: *Race Relations* (New York: Oxford University Press, 1971); and R. W. Mack, ed.: *Race, Class, and Power* (New York: Van Nostrand Reinhold, 1968).

Index